RURAL WORKER ADJUSTMENT TO URBAN LIFE

An Assessment of the Research

POLICY PAPERS IN HUMAN RESOURCES
AND INDUSTRIAL RELATIONS 15

Varden Fuller

THE INSTITUTE OF LABOR AND

INDUSTRIAL RELATIONS

THE UNIVERSITY OF MICHIGAN

WAYNE STATE UNIVERSITY

A JOINT PUBLICATION WITH THE

NATIONAL MANPOWER POLICY TASK FORCE

INSTITUTE OF LABOR AND INDUSTRIAL RELATIONS

All Americans have a vital stake in the shaping of sound public and private industrial relations policies and in the expansion of pertinent knowledge and skills. The Institute of Labor and Industrial Relations is a joint agency of The University of Michigan (Ann Arbor) and Wayne State University (Detroit). It was established in the spring of 1957 in order to maximize the contribution of each University, in activities related to industrial relations, to the people of Michigan and to the educational and research needs of workers and management.

The Institute has three major functions: first, to facilitate regular university instruction in the disciplines and professions related to industrial relations; second, to encourage basic and applied research on industrial relations topics; and third, to organize and promote programs of community education in industrial relations designed to serve labor, management and the public.

CHARLES M. REHMUS
Co-Director
The University of Michigan
Ann Arbor

RONALD W. HAUGHTON
Co-Director
Wayne State University
Detroit

NATIONAL MANPOWER POLICY TASK FORCE

A private nonprofit organization for studies and research in manpower policy.

Curtis Aller
San Francisco State University

Garth L. Mangum
University of Utah

E. Wight Bakke
Yale University

F. Ray Marshall
University of Texas

Lisle Carter
Cornell University

Charles A. Myers, Chairman
Massachusetts Institute of Technology

Rashi Fein
Harvard University

Albert Rees
Princeton University

Eli Ginzberg
Columbia University

R. Thayne Robson
University of Utah

Frederick H. Harbison
Princeton University

Gerald G. Somers
University of Wisconsin

Vivian Henderson
Clark College

M. H. Trytten
National Academy of Sciences

Myron Joseph
Carnegie–Mellon University

Lloyd Ulman
University of California, Berkeley

Charles C. Killingsworth
Michigan State University

Sar A. Levitan, Vice–Chairman
The George Washington University

Lowell M. Glenn
Executive Director

RURAL WORKER ADJUSTMENT TO URBAN LIFE
An Assessment of the Research

Varden Fuller
UNIVERSITY OF CALIFORNIA, BERKELEY

A JOINT PUBLICATION OF THE

INSTITUTE OF LABOR AND INDUSTRIAL RELATIONS

THE UNIVERSITY OF MICHIGAN — WAYNE STATE UNIVERSITY

AND THE

NATIONAL MANPOWER POLICY TASK FORCE

WASHINGTON, D.C.

ANN ARBOR, MICHIGAN

FEBRUARY 1970

This research was prepared under a contract with the
Office of Manpower Research, Manpower Administration,
United States Department of Labor, under the authority
of the Manpower Development and Training Act. Researchers
undertaking such projects with Government sponsorship
are encouraged to express their own judgment freely.
Therefore, points of view or opinions stated in this
document do not necessarily represent the official
position or policy of the Department of Labor.

CONTENTS

1

INTRODUCTION

Central to this essay is the significant question – incredibly late in coming into public awareness – how well has the rural labor force adjusted to the urban setting? At best the rural-urban dichotomy is hazy. Nevertheless, much widely divergent research has been associated with it, however imprecisely. A reviewer of research has to establish terminal boundaries for his work and in this instance – with a vague central concept and an array of no less vague peripheral associations – the cutoff boundaries have had to be rather arbitrary. Consequently, not everyone will find that specific areas or items in which he is interested have been considered.

This is not a literature of affirmation. It deals with a grim but impassively suffered episode in our national life. The research contributions concerning it are fragmental, superficial, and generally unsatisfying.

The rural-to-urban movement in American socioeconomic history is one of dual mischance. Farm people were pushed off farms and cities were agglomerated, both as by-products of forces not clearly perceived and without benefit of articulated purpose. No deliberately formulated objective was served at either end of this disorderly transaction. Contemporary writers are fond of saying that farm technological advance made a great contribution to national welfare by freeing a labor force to serve the growing manpower needs of the nonfarm economy. To say that much is to state a truism, provided one accepts the inherent assumption that the expanded nonfarm economy has been a national blessing. But to go further, as is done, and imply that the release of farm manpower was the intended objective of farm technological advance is to place rationalization upon what was only the fortuitous result of a disorderly episode. If moving manpower from the farms had been deliberate, something would have been done to develop this resource and prepare for its effective utilization in the nonfarm world. The facts are to the contrary — miserably so. Off-farm movers have been required to adjust alone, often against bewildering and frustrating obstacles.

When the U. S. Department of Agriculture and the Land-Grant College system was initiated just over 100 years ago, it was with the anticipation that, if farmers could be helped to be more productive they would prosper and the foundations of Jeffersonian rural life would be strengthened. It was a populist and rural fundamentalist idea. But contrary to expectation, the Land-Grant College Act was to become probably the most influential prometropolitan step ever undertaken by any national government.

The expected new farm technology did materialize, though not immediately and not entirely as a result of the public effort. By helping to make food abundant and moderately priced, it contributed much to the American people. However, for farmers it contributed more to their obsolescence than to their prosperity.

In the past twenty years, the amount of labor required for farming has declined by 4.7 percent per year, the farm population by 4.3 percent per year. These rates of adjustment have brought revolutionary changes in the lives of millions. That government should continue to support farm technological advance as well as to subsidize the price-depressing consequences of surplus production was not seriously questioned; that government might assume some responsibility for those being technologically disrupted was never seriously debated until embraced in the broader consciousness of the Manpower Development and Training Act of 1962. No real money has ever been spent on research concerning human adjustments of ex-farm people or on aiding those adjustments.

If the magnitude of disruption absorbed by the farm population had occurred in the more cohesive and articulated groupings of factory situations, the response might well have been less impassive and consequently the obligation to adjust might not have been left so exclusively to the individual.

However, a few voices were heard to question whether the massive rural-to-urban adjustment was being as successful as it seemed for either the populations involved, the communities of exodus, or the communities of relocation. That underemployment, unemployment, and poverty were persistently rural as well as urban could be known by those who wished to know. Much of what superficially seemed to be urban assimilation was only tentative emulsion; much of what seemed to be rural accommodation was only the extraordinary capacity of rural people to adjust to varying forms and intensities of underemployment.

Concern about the rural-urban population adjustment was very late in coming. Meanwhile, unsolved rural poverty problems were flowing into urban ghettos and there being transmuted into the second and third generations. Others, not relocating in urban places, were the "people left behind" of whom fourteen million were found by the President's National Advisory Commission on Rural Poverty in 1967 to be in poverty. Neither the lateness of the Rural Poverty Commission and the Commission on Civil Disorders nor the scale of subsequent response to their recommendations stands as testimonial to governmental perception in the absence of massive political pressure.

Before the mid-1960's, there was very little governmental interest in the rural labor force. Consequently, the meager research support available was oriented more to academic disciplinary interests than to "practical" matters. The principal source was the USDA-Agricultural Experiment Station funding, from which cooperative projects (usually small) could be supported between USDA and academic discipline-oriented workers in the State Experiment Stations. These agricultural fund sources enabled the development of a fair sum of knowledge concerning farm labor requirements, efficiency of labor use, underemployment, and the interrelations between these and changing technology. Agricultural funds supported the Census-USDA series on farm population and hired labor force as well as the USDA's series on farm wages and employment, in addition to numerous studies in demography, mobility, rural community development, levels of living, and related subjects. Additionally, agricultural funds were the principal support for rural sociologists who virtually alone were interested in the assimilation of off-farm migrants and in the impacts felt by the communities of exodus and of entry.

In contrast, knowledge of the nonfarm labor force in the rural sector is almost totally lacking—that population has not had the homogeneity, power, and articulation essential to achieving identity or attention.

Notwithstanding its fragmented and dominantly academic character, the economic and sociological research relating to farm manpower has had some value in policy-making, and perhaps, the most outstanding instance is the series of cooperative USDA-State Experiment Station studies in the early 1950's on the preparedness of farmers to retire, which undoubtedly influenced the legislative decision to remove the exclusion of farmers from Social Security coverage.[1] *

The most serious defects of the research in this general area have been overaggregation and fragmentation. For instance, it took agricultural economists years to discover that apparently irrational behavior by off-farm migrants (in deciding when to move) was irrational only in the light of the economist's own propensity to homogenize diverse circumstances by assuming away regional and other heterogeneities. At the other extreme, many studies of assimilation have been so small and so particular that they lacked capacity for generalization.

There are at least two hindrances to acquiring useful information in this area. One is that, in contrast to an ever more rapidly changing world, statistical processes have become slower and consequently, data are obsolete before they become available. This is more a matter of uncertain financial support than of statistical technology. Another is the inherent disciplinary insulation between economists and sociologists. Their respective theorems, perceptions, and approaches to the adjustment process have never been effectively joined; consequently, their results have not been much more addable than are elephants and chickens. In the application (or testing) of academic theorems,

*Notes are at the end of each chapter.

concern has been with one aspect or another—the whole of the process was not brought under purview.

The prevailing notion of how people leave the land has probably been overinfluenced by Steinbeck's Joad family and other similar literary characters. True enough, the current migration to the North and West out of the rural deep South has some characteristics similar to the "Okie-Arkie" migration to California in the 1930's which *The Grapes of Wrath* made famous. Nevertheless, the great bulk of the movement out of agriculture has been less dramatic. Not always has it involved an entire family, an abrupt separation from the farm, or the loading of portable goods upon an old car and heading down the road—or, as now, catching the bus to Chicago with a ticket provided by a relative or friend already there.

Several quite distinct categories of rural human resource adjustment need to be recognized. The largest of all is the youth of the farm families, many of whom have performed chores or done summer work on the family farm while growing up, but who effectively started their working careers elsewhere. Where industry has expanded into rural areas, youth can enter nonfarm occupations while living at home, and their ultimate settlement upon being married may not take them out of the county or state. It may be that the exceptional attention given by rural sociologists to departing farm youth is a reflection of deep-rooted and possibly subconscious agrarian fundamentalism. To stay in the home community and in the father's occupation is not the usual practice in modern society.

Industrial expansion into rural areas, together with the building of commutable highways, has facilitated job mobility by established farmers, while easing the requirement of residence migration. Particularly in the Northeast and North Central regions, the pattern of farm size has, under farm technological advance, become too small to keep the typical operator more than partly employed. In the absence of nearby industrial employment opportunities, there would have been great pressure to make a full break with farming and to migrate. In a suitable environment, part-time farming has been a nondisruptive and quite painless adjustment, especially for those young enough to be acceptable to nonfarm employers and with enough energy to "moonlight" the farm with the help of children still at home. In the agricultural economics literature, this arrangement is usually regarded as transitional migration, ultimately ending in a full separation from farming. However, in practicable locations, a pattern of small farm living-commuting-nonfarm employment may prove viable and attractive. Even if the combination persists, its total magnitude has severe constraints.

Another large and heterogeneous category of rural-urban adjustment is hired farm labor—regularly hired, seasonally hired, and migratory. Excepting "plight" studies of migratory workers, this category gets little attention—research or otherwise. Nevertheless, occupational adjustments are occurring in this category that warrant acknowledgment even though they have not attracted much research interest.

Farm owners and the tenant operators who are not able to enter part-time farming or to make an occupational change without leaving agriculture and usually also migration face drastic occupational and social adjustments. If the person is a tenant, the severance can quite readily be made—leases are terminated and equipment sold, provided the tenant is a commercial farmer and not a sharecropper (the latter have special problems of getting away—mainly indebtedness to the plantation owner). In the ongoing process of farm consolidation, tenancy operations are terminated, and the land is leased to nearby owners (thereby making bigger operating units). The Census category "full owners" still accounts for most farms—since 1910, just over half of all farms. The category "part owner" (owners who lease additional land) has risen as tenants have declined. The implication is that land formerly operated by farmers who were wholly tenants is being taken over by established owners. In 1964, full owners were 57 percent of all operators and part owners were 25 percent, but the percentages of farm land controlled were respectively 29 and 48.[2] Tenants are rapidly disappearing, but American agrarian fundamentalism has seldom recognized their existence and then with lament, so there is very little research or political interest in their situation.

Fulltime farmers who are owners of all or part of their land are found to have the lowest occupational and residence mobility of any of the farm population. This is partly a matter of age and family and community ties as well as land ownership. As an incidental point, the expectation of further capital gains in land values has been found to be one of the deterrents to off-farm mobility.

The reason for detail in the immediately preceding comments on categories of off-farm occupational adjustment is to emphasize that, even when stated in broad terms that ignore important regional, ethnic, type-of-farming, and similar differences, off-farm adjustment is still a multifaceted complex, and it is one in which distinctions among economic development, mobility, migrancy, and just plain growing up are not readily maintained.

Nearly nothing is known about the rural nonfarm population, and what we know is obtained mainly from subtraction, first of the urban and then of the farm populations. Demographers can determine some of the vital statistics of this arithmetic residual, but very little that is meaningful can be extracted. To be nonurban and nonfarm is little more than to be nonpeople. Although there are economic activities in nonurban areas other than farming, we know virtually nothing of the occupational interrelations among these and the farms and the metropolitan centers. The rural nonfarm activity has undoubtedly played a role, perhaps mostly transitional, in off-farm adjustment. But of the extent and character of that role, very little is known. Farm and nonfarm youth do share one supremely important attribute — they must all have been products of the same inferior school systems and, therefore, have the same basic ill-preparedness to cope with urban and modern industrial demands.

The generality of my opening statement concerning the rural-urban dichotomy as a research perspective needs specification. That I believe it has not been a fruitful perspective, that I believe it has obscured the perception of more important attributes in human development — are allegations concerning the past on which the value of argument is doubtful. Given the historical determinism of the dichotomy, there probably was little choice. But for the future, I would definitely argue against a perspective of rural versus urban as regards manpower, mobility, or occupational adjustment research.

We *are* an urban society; the questions for the future are not urban *versus* rural but rather *what kind of urban*. Obviously, the concept of urban implied is not density of settlement or distance away from a metropolitan center but rather the quality of urbaneness in the population. Even though the hinterlands are likely to remain, it is not to be assumed or expected that they will (or ought to!) be inhabited by hinterlandish people, for whom hinterlandish institutions of human development are sufficient.[3]

Consequently, for the future, fruitful research in the area of rural-urban adjustment should, in my view, start from a view of persons with equal potential (that is, equal inherent capacity, equal values, equal motivations) who inhabit a socioeconomic system of unequal access (to opportunities and privileges, including principally those of preparation and development).

From that perspective, obstacles to adjustment should be clearer, and whatever corrections the political system is able to make should be less faltering.

NOTES

1. Some examples: Walter C. McKain, Jr., Elmer D. Baldwin, and Louis J. Ducoff, *Old Age and Retirement in Rural Connecticut,* Connecticut Agricultural Experiment Station Bul. 299 (Storrs, 1953), 51p.; William H. Sewell, Charles E. Ramsey, and Louis J. Ducoff, *Farmers' Conception and Plans for Economic Security in Old Age,* Wisconsin Agricultural Experiment Station Research Bul. 182 (Madison, 1953), 22p.
2. U.S. Bureau of the Census, *U.S. Census of Agriculture; 1964,* Vol. II, General Report, Chapter 8, pp. 763-64.
3. If my terms seem to be murky, the brief discussion of a proposed new hinterland ecology as a substitute for traditional rurality in the following section may clarify.

2

CONCEPTS, DEFINITIONS, AND MAGNITUDES

In simpler times, President Theodore Roosevelt could appoint a Country Life Commission (1908) without leaving much doubt as to what segment of society he had in mind. Country meant rural; rural meant farm; the people living on farms were the farmers; and country, rural, and farm were synonyms. Even if this image was always somewhat ideological, it was valid enough for ordinary communication in those times.

Today, four out of five rural residents are not engaged in farming; two out of five gainfully employed residents of farms do no farm work or very little; and one out of three persons employed at farm work does not live on a farm. Yet, the vestiges of old images and expressions persist; and typically, when rural-urban relationships are spoken of, the implicit reference is to those "down on the farm" or, in the instances of "rural-urban migration," those who are leaving farms to move somewhere else, presumably, into an urban setting.

Six decades after Theodore Roosevelt's Country Life Commission, President Lyndon Johnson appointed a National Advisory Commission on Rural Poverty (1966). His executive order did not define "rural"; but in using that term, it speaks of rural life, areas, economic development, and labor. Only for "rural labor" does it add the phrase "including farm labor."[1] Accordingly, the 1966 Commission appropriately took its mandate as including nonfarm as well as farm people. Hence, the now generally prevailing concept that rural means everybody who is not urban became the implicit definition for the 1966 Rural Poverty Commission.[2]

In an effort to be more precise, government statistics divide the rural sector into farm and nonfarm components. Additionally, the definition of what constitutes a farm is somewhat less inclusive and subjective than formerly. Consequently, there is a degree of homogeneity in the concept and measurement of "rural-farm." Nevertheless, the definition is woefully lacking as an accurate measure of farm labor force or farm employment.

Perhaps the best that can be said for the rural-farm concept is that it is not worse than "urban" and a lot better than "rural nonfarm." The latter is truly a heterogeneous residual — it is the remainder of what is not urban and not farm. It includes small towns, villages, hamlets, open country (other than farm), and all sorts of "fringes" to places classifiable as urban.

The Census tells us something about the occupations that are found among rural residents but little of rural economies other than agriculture. What is urban and what is rural is primarily a matter of *residence density* which may not be closely correlated with intensity of *economic activity* and need not be correlated at all with any particular content of economic activity.

Researchers have usually wanted to be able to say how specifically rural a particular area was. Sociologists would apparently have preferred to be able to measure attitudes — values, beliefs, solidarities, and roles.[3] Economists have sometimes developed indexes of rurality depending upon proportions of employment in farming. The authors of *People of Rural America* (one sociologist and two agricultural economists) have based what is probably the most functionally realistic measure of rurality[4] on a hinterland concept — the farther from an urban center one is, the more hinterlandish and, therefore, the more rural.

> In essence, rural America is regarded as representing the hinterland of a series of metropolitan regions. The rural portions of the Nation are viewed as being interdependent with the metropolitan centers, but the power to intergrate, order, and control resides in the large centers. This concept of the ecological structure as ap-

plied to rural areas supersedes the long-held view of numerous local, relatively self-sufficient rural communities as the most significant natural entities blanketing the Nation.[5]

The total population defined as rural has remained substantially constant at around fifty million since 1910, a constancy that in itself has no particular meaning, for within these decades the rural population has undergone immense internal changes in (1) its occupational distribution and (2) its geographic locations. During the 1950's, almost one-half of the nation's counties lost population; of those counties that were entirely rural and dominated by agriculture (approximately one-third of all counties), three-fourths were depopulating. At the opposite extreme, of those counties that were primarily urban, only one-sixth declined.[6]

Although our knowledge about this subject is fragmented and weakly aggregated, the valid inferences are clearly that agriculture contributed heavily (and in some areas, dominantly) to urban growth in recent decades. In 1958, approximately five-eights of all farm-born adults (18 years and over) were no longer living on farms. There was some offset to this, however, because against the 16,348,000 who had left farm residence, 2,584,000 nonfarm born (including foreign-born) were counted in the adult farm population which, in 1958, was at a total of 12,035,000. Of the 16,348,000 adult farm-born migrants, ten percent had, at some time in their lives, established a nonfarm residence and then moved back to a farm.[7]

As is indicated by estimates yet to be considered, the magnitude of off-farm movements has been sustained through this decade to date, even as the residual base for migration diminished (that is, the rate has increased). Consequently, the proportion of farm-reared adults now alive but no longer living on farms probably exceeds three-fourths. These off-farm emigrees are now probably not less than one-fifth of the total adult nonfarm population.

The national statistical measure most commonly used to describe the magnitude and rate of off-farm adjustment of the farm work force is the Census-USDA series on *farm population*.[8] However, since people can be and are farm residents without being employed in agriculture, this does not measure the farm labor force. Moreover, since the proportion of farm residents employed in nonfarm work is rising, it is not precisely indicative of changes in farm employment. Reciprocally, an increasing proportion of those doing farm work do not live on farms. In Tables 1A and 1B, note that the numbers of farm residents engaged in nonfarm work stayed substantially unchanged from 1960 to 1966, while a sharp decrease occurred in the number of farm residents doing farm work. Reciprocally, nonfarm residents employed in agriculture remained fairly stable. Hence, in both respects, it was the off-farm movement of farm-employed manpower that changed the proportions.[9]

It is generally believed that farmers are moving their residences to nearby towns while continuing to farm and that hired farm laborers also are shifting away from on-farm living. However, since the number of on-farm-occupied persons declined by 1,131,000 in the years 1960-66 whereas the farm-employed persons not living on farms increased by only 91,000 in the same period, it would appear that very little of the off-farm movement is explainable as off-farm relocation without change of occupation. Obversely, these data suggest that the great majority of off-farm movers were simultaneously changing domicile and occupation. In this period, the decline of 1,131,000 in the farm-occupied, on-farm residents was matched approximately by a decline of 1,040,000 in total agricultural employment.

Statistical series on farm labor force or on agricultural employment depend upon numerous, quite arbitrary definitions. This is because people otherwise employed or not otherwise in the labor market do much of the seasonal farm work, and because farmers also frequently have dual occupations.

Table 1A *Employment Status of the Farm Population 14 Years Old and Over, 1960 and 1966[a]*

	1960		1966	
	Number	Percent	Number	Percent
	1,000		1,000	
Labor force status				
Employed	6,089	97.2	4,811	98.3
Agriculture	4,025	64.2	2,894	59.1
Nonagriculture	2,064	33.0	1,917	39.2
Unemployed	177	2.8	85	1.7
Total in labor force (both sexes)	6,266	100.0	4,896	100.0

a. Observations are in April.

Table 1B *Agricultural Employment of the Farm and Nonfarm Population 14 Years Old and Over, 1960 and 1966*[a]

	1960		1966	
	Number	Percent	Number	Percent
	1,000		1,000	
Residence				
Farm	4,025	74.6	2,894	66.5
Nonfarm	1,370	25.4	1,461	33.5
Total employed (both sexes)	5,395	100.0	4,355	100.0

a. Observations are in April.
Source: U. S. Bureau of the Census and U.S. Economic Research Service, *Farm Population*, Series Census—ERS (P-27), No. 37, April 1967, pp. 3, 4.

Under these circumstances, there are two general choices upon which estimates may be based: (1) count as the farm labor force those whose chief activity is farm employment (which greatly understates the number of persons involved) or (2) count all who did *some* (any at all or a minimum amount of) farm work (which overstates the effective labor force).

The U.S. Department of Agriculture has maintained the oldest and most widely used farm employment series which is based essentially on the latter alternative. Its annual estimates are averages of monthly estimates and, hence, end up being much below the total number of persons involved in the peak months of activity and above the numbers in the months of slack activity. For *magnitudes*, Agriculture's employment series has no definite or determinable meaning; but, having been maintained on a fairly homogeneous statistical system over the years, it is valid for indicating directions and rate of *change*.

Trying to infer occupational adjustment from changes in residence is not the happiest world for a researcher for the reasons already mentioned; trying to infer occupational mobility from changes in the aggregate level of farm employment is no more satisfactory. One needs to know something of the characteristics of identified persons and populations in their prior and subsequent occupational situations—the more details, the better. Not until Social Security coverage was extended to farmers and farm laborers in the 1950's was there a national source of such data. Conceptually, the continuous registry of identifiable individuals' work history over a series of years is an ideal way of measuring off-farm occupational adjustment. However, as we shall note subsequently, these data with respect to their farm-nonfarm indications have proven somewhat intractable.

As further background of this introductory review, some of the basic magnitudes are drawn together in Table 2. Over the quarter century with which we are most concerned, the national agricultural plant has functioned on a fairly stable but gradually diminishing acreage of harvested cropland, ranging from 350 to 290 million acres. Farm population has fallen by almost two-thirds; farm employment and the number of farms have decreased by one-half; and net output is approaching a jump of three-fourths. In the aggregate, these data reflect the dramatic magnitude of human adjustment which has been concentrated within the post-World War II years. With even more intense changes in many counties and communities, it is remarkable that so much has occurred so quietly.

Two main factors are involved in the rising farm output per acre and per man: (1) new technology to increase the effectiveness of land and labor, and (2) the transfer of farm activities to industrial sites; for example, tractors and petroleum for horsepower and animal feed, packing and processing plants in place of farm packing and processing; and chemical fertilizer in place of animal-produced fertilizer. In effect, this means that a very large percentage of erstwhile farm work is no longer done on farms.

The peak of farm population was reached in 1916. Although observers in prior years were aware of the exodus of young people from farms and considered it "inevitable and justified,"[10] it was not until the decade 1920-30 that net off-farm migration reached a volume that almost offset the net natural increase of the farm population (see Table 3). As an aggregate for the decade, the same cancellation effect prevailed through the 1930's.[11] Beginning with the 1940's and persisting since, average annual net off-farm migration (all persons) has typically been 800,000 to 1,000,000 per year. Over the same time span, average annual net natural increase has fallen consistently, from approximately 4000,000 in 1930-49 to 90,000 in 1965-66. The result is that off-farm migration since 1940 has more than cancelled natural increase; it has cut deeply into the capital population (compare columns 4, 5, and 6 of Table 3).

Table 2 *Some Basic Magnitudes and Trends Relating to Farm Manpower Adjustment, 1930-66*

Year	Farm population[a]	Farm employment	Number of farms	Net farm production index (1957-59 = 100)
	million persons		million	
1930	30.5	12.5	6.3	62.0
1935	32.2	12.7	6.8	61.5
1940	30.5	11.0	6.1	69.8
1945	24.4	10.0	5.9	83.6
1950	21.9	9.9	5.4	84.4
1955	19.1	8.4	4.8	97.6
1960	15.6	7.1	3.7[b]	105.9
1961	14.8	6.9		104.6
1962	14.3	6.7		107.0
1963	13.4	6.5		111.6
1964	12.9	6.1	3.2[b]	112.5
1965	12.4	5.6		116.6
1966[c]	11.6	5.2		112.7

a. All persons.
b. Preceding year.
c. For April 1968, the farm population was 10.4 million, or 5.2 percent of total population (data from Census-ERS Series P-27, July 31, 1969). At the rate of reduction prevailing through the 1960's, the percentage of the national population living on farms will decline from 8.7 in 1960 to 4.5 in 1970, a reduction in proportion of 50 percent. The reduction in absolute numbers of farm population is likely to be near 40 percent.
Source: U.S. Department of Agriculture, *Agricultural Statistics, 1967*, pp. 510, 526, 528, and 541.

Quite obviously, given the diminished size of the on-farm population, its declining reproductive potential, and currently prevailing high rates of migration, the epoch of intense farm exodus must terminate sometime soon. As the approach of a plateau becomes apparent — surely not later than the mid-1970's — (assuming that the definitions of "farm" and "farm population" do not change substantially), it appears that the farm population not engaged in farming as its principal activity will soon come to exceed the farm population actually engaged in farming. Reciprocally, it appears not unlikely that the major portion of those employed in agriculture will be nonfarm residents. The traditional concepts of rural-farm separateness from the rest of society will then be truly defunct.

Table 3 *United States Farm Population: Changes, 1920-66, with Effects of Natural Increase and Off-Farm Migration*

Time period	Average farm population for period	Average natural increase per year	Average net off-farm migration per year	Natural increase	Net off-farm migration	Net off-farm migration minus natural increase[a]
	1	2	3	4	5	6
					Percentages of average population for period	
	1,000				percent	
1920-29	31,270	485	630	1.6	2.0	0.5
1930-39	31,444	385	383	1.2	1.2	0.0
1940-49	26,481	390	1,139	1.5	4.3	2.8
1950-59	19,475	271	1,013	1.4	5.2	3.8
1960-61	15,219	162	823	1.1	5.4	4.3
1962-63	13,84.	140	1,086	1.0	7.8	6.2
1965-66	11,979	90	858	0.7	7.2	6.4
1967-68	10,665	60	481	0.6	4.5	4.0

a. Column 3 minus column 2 divided by column 1.
Source: From or based upon U.S. Economic Research Service, *Farm Population Estimates for 1910-1962*, ERS-130, p. 23, and subsequent annual issues.

NOTES

1. *The People Left Behind*, A Report by the President's National Advisory Commission on Rural Poverty (Washington, D.C., 1967), p. vi.
2. *Ibid.*, p. 3
3. Fern K. Willits and Robert C. Bealer, "An Evaluation of a Composite Definition of Rurality," *Rural Sociology*, Vol. 32, No. 2 (June 1967), pp. 165-77.
   Leo F. Schnore, "The Rural-Urban Variable: An Urbanite's Perspective," *Rural Sociology*, Vol. 31, No. 2 (June 1966).
4. U.S. Bureau of the Census, *People of Rural America*, A 1960 Census Monograph, by Dale E. Hathaway, J. Allan Beegle, and W. Keith Bryant, 1968, p. 289.
5. *Ibid.*, pp. 1,2.
6. Calvin L. Beale, "Rural Depopulation in the United States: Some Demographic Consequences of Agricultural Adjustments," *Demography*, Vol. 1, No. 1, 1964.
   Louis J. Ducoff, "Changing Occupations and Levels of Living of Rural People," Paper read before the 40th Annual Agricultural Outlook Conference, Washington, D.C., November 14, 1962 (U.S. Economic Research Service, 1962), p. 21.
7. "Between 1940 and 1954, an estimated one-half of the expansion in the nonagricultural labor force was supplied by migration from the farm population and one-half of this was from low-income farming areas." See Ducoff, "Trends and Characteristics of Farm Population in Low-Income Farming Areas," *Journal of Farm Economics*, Vol. XXXVII, No. 5 (December 1955), p. 1407. The 1958 data are from Calvin L. Beale, John C. Hudson, and Vera J. Banks, *Characteristics of the U.S. Population by Farm and Nonfarm Origin*, U.S. Economic Research Service, Agricultural Economics Report No. 66, 1964.
8. "Farm population" is defined as being residents of a farm or ranch. Criteria of what constitutes such a unit have differed through the years. For a discussion of the changes and their effects, see Vera J. Banks, Calvin L. Beale, and Gladys K. Bowles, *Farm Population Estimates for 1910-1962*, U.S. Economic Research Service, ERS-130, October 1963, p. 49; and U.S. Bureau of the Census and U.S. Economic Research Service, *Farm Population*, Series Census—AMS (p. 27), no. 28.
9. This point warrants emphasis because it does happen that the shifting proportions will be interpreted to mean that more and more farmers are changing occupations without moving off their farm, which is not so even though the percentage increased.
10. Beale, "Rural Depopulation . . .," *op. cit.*, p. 265.
11. There was net in-migration in several years as unemployed returned to farms.

3

THE BASIC EXPELLANT:
AGRICULTURAL
TECHNOLOGICAL ADVANCE

Dating primarily from 1950, a considerable body of research literature has been developed which deals with technological change in agriculture — rising labor productivity, the demand for farm labor, the level of farm employment (including underemployment), and the interrelations among these variables. Even without this literature, the aware citizen would have been conscious of the virtually truistic main finding of those writings — namely, that career and employment opportunities in farming have been sharply declining. Former farm residents in urban populations, including relatives and friends, are sources of lay information on individual situations and experiences, including explanations as to why some farm youths did not enter farm careers and why some farmers have quit, and why some have returned to farming. While the lay information may have lacked ultimate explanatory sophistication, it has been sufficiently communicative to instill the understanding that the departure from farms was not entirely a matter of freely elected preference for urban life and nonfarm occupations.

For the individual farmer, farm youth, or hired worker, technological change is encountered in price (wage) and income terms—very few have simply been replaced by a machine, as might happen in a factory or mine or in construction. Direct displacement has occurred, as in cotton picking and other hand-harvest activities, but since the workers were generally seasonal or migratory, they had no established job rights and no firm employment relationships from which to be separated. Direct displacement has also occurred for sharecroppers and tenants when landlords needed their land to use new machinery effectively.

In terms of the impact of changing technology upon their situation, wage laborers and sharecroppers have been little noticed. In contrast, the cost-price squeeze dilemma, which for present or would-be individual farm entrepreneurs is the central impact of technological change, is well and widely known—to bankers, politicians, researchers, and citizens generally.

A parenthetical point to be noted is that the cost-price squeeze of the 1950's and 1960's has been comparatively free of the harshness of foreclosure and bankruptcy that was so characteristic of earlier decades. This difference results from the fact that technological change, while decreasing the demand for labor, has increased the demand for land; with an intense demand for land, farmers could terminate with income or capital gains from renting or selling their land, and thereby depart solvently, and often comfortably. This also has been one pleasant factor in the choice of farm-inheriting offspring who decided not to continue in their fathers' occupation.

When this nation committed itself to promoting technological progress in agriculture—by the Morrill (Land-Grant College) Act in 1862 and the Smith-Lever (Agricultural Extension) Act in 1914, the then distant outcome which has only recently been realized, was completely unanticipated. The expectation was that the farmers would prosper if they could be shown how to be more efficient. Economic analysis, which is now sufficiently endowed with theory and empirical coefficients to explain approximately what happened, was not then (and may not be yet) sufficiently equipped to identify and project the impacts of technological change. Agricultural economists and the body of knowledge they have developed arrived on the scene only in time to demonstrate that the miscarriage of the dream of millions of farmers being made ever more prosperous by higher orders of productive efficiency was not due to sinister political forces but only the rational outcome of invincible economic laws.

The generally accepted measures of technological and

productivity changes and their interrelations with aggregate farm labor requirements are well summarized by Walter R. Butcher in work done for the National Commission on Technology, Automation, and Economic Progress.[1] The basic facts correlate with, and implicitly explain, the reductions in farm population and labor force that were mentioned in the preceding section.

Gross factor productivity, i.e., output in ratio to all inputs, has risen sharply and continuously since 1920. Even more spectacularly, the charted indexes of total labor input and of output per man-hour have diverged at almost right angles since 1940. If agricultural output had faced an indefinitely expansible market, total production could have been more greatly increased and thereby enabled the retention of a greater proportion of the earlier farm labor force. But the market had not had sufficient absorptive capacity to offset gains in productivity; consequently, the intermediating mechanism relating increases in productivity to labor force adjustments has been the generally adverse farm price and income outlook. Given this outlook, thousands of farm youth have had to decide, individually, whether to stay with the family occupation, and fewer thousands of farmers have had to decide, also individually, whether to continue. This decision-making process is quite different from that of a few large industrial managements, each of which makes a single decision affecting the careers of thousands of workers.

Measures and concepts of productivity are seldom as self-evident as they appear. The widely quoted indexes of farm output — total and per man-hour — obscure the fact that over the years inputs utilized on the farm have increasingly been produced by labor employed off the farm. At the other end of the process, preparing, packaging, and marketing activities that formerly were done on the farm have been transferred to off-farm industries. Consequently, the work done on the farm has been foreshortened both ways. Nevertheless, the ratios in common use attribute the raw product only to that labor employed on farms and hence exaggerate rises in farm labor productivity.

 An inherent problem that plagues the makers of indexes of change in productivity is the difficulty of maintaining homogeneity in time series when large changes are occurring in products as well as in processes. Since farm products have remained fairly homogeneous, it is mainly on the input side that measurement of agricultural productivity changes become elusive.

In a recent and sophisticated analysis, Folke Dovring employed the concept of aggregated labor to overcome some of the limitations of the above-described gross or partial productivity ratios.[2] His aggregates included nonfarm labor used to produce and service production requisites as well as the direct labor used on farms. Inputs usually incorporated in gross productivity measures, such as land rent, interest on capital, and property taxes, are excluded in the Dovring analysis. Consequently, with respect to labor use, all farms and their suppliers are treated as a subsystem of the economy. Dovring found that indirect labor had remained fairly stable at 1.5 million to 2 million man-years from 1919-65, but that "industries and services supplying farm requisites have increased their productivity to such a degree that they have been able to supply a vastly increased physical volume of goods and services without using up any correspondingly increased portion of the nation's work force."[3]

Gross on-farm labor productivity ratios incorporate and reflect these off-farm productivity gains. They also incorporate the effects of other inputs that are not usually accounted for, including government services affecting knowledge, education, health, and the quality of the production environment.

Workers employed on farms are unquestionably able to work more effectively than formerly, but this has happened only as part of a comprehensive transformation in which society at large has participated. Viewing the process in these broader terms, Dovring found that the acceleration in agriculture productivity started not in 1940, but in 1919.

Perhaps if researchers had been able to provide an earlier and clearer vision of the comprehensive technological process, the formation of government policy for agriculture could have centered more appropriately on facilitating manpower adjustment rather than upon futile efforts to reshape price and market structures.

In any event, the farm manpower adjustment process is not yet complete. Reciprocally, as the voluminous documentation of the urban crisis testifies, substantial portions of the first, second, and third generations of off-farm migrants are still in an unstable state of nonassimilation. Evidence that further off-farm movement is yet impending is supplied by a recent research report for the North Central region.[4] In this work, projections were made of the minimum cost (i.e., optimum resource use) and market-clearing reorganization of farms in 1980 — a state reflecting the economists' concept of equilibrium. To achieve this by 1980 would require fewer and larger farms, less labor, and less capital than were reported by the Census for 1959 (and most certainly less than will be reported for 1969). Numbers of farms would have to continue to decline at the observed rate for 1949-59; labor (all inputs at the farm level) "would require a constant accrual percentage decrease equal to that observed in the 1939-59 period."[5] At the projected 1980 adjustment for this region, there would be 350,000 farms compared with over 1.1 million in 1959.

The North Central region may not be completely representative of all other regions. Nevertheless, there is probably no region that has reached its plateau of farm adjustment; the unknowns relate not to direction of change but to future rates and final plateaus.

NOTES

1. Walter R. Butcher, *The Employment Impact of Technological Change,* Appendix Volume II, Studies prepared for the National Commission on Technology, Automation, and Economic Progress (Washington, D.C., 1966), pp. 141-52.
2. Folke Dovring, *Productivity of Labor in Agricultural Production,* Illinois Agricultural Experiment Station Bulletin 726 (Urbana, 1967).
3. *Ibid.,* p. 13.
4. *Efficient Organization of the Farm Industry in the North Central Region of the United States in 1959 and 1980,* Iowa Agriculture and Home Economics Experiment Station, Research Bulletin 560 (Ames, 1968).
5. *Ibid.,* p. 110.

4

OPPORTUNITIES AND UNCERTAINTIES IN THE ECONOMIC ENVIRONMENT

In the history of American off-farm migration, 1942 was monumental. In that year, the net out-movement was four to five times that of the average of the late 1930's and 1940. The other two years of defense and war build-up — 1941 and 1943 — were also exceptionally large at two to three times the prewar levels. By 1944, the off-farm movement had declined to its prewar normal of approximately three-quarter million. The first inversion since 1932-33 came in 1945, with a net inflow to farms of 670,000.[1]

For all that could be known then, 1945 might have been the initiation of a prolonged back-to-the-farm movement. But, "as the ball bounced," it has so far stood alone as a modern year of net reverse flow.

The year 1945 was one of massive uncertainty. Termination of the war was expected. War industries and their newly built communities were not expected to make an effective transition to peacetime prosperity. Since the prewar New Deal had never solved the unemployment problem, much of the adult population had little reason to be optimistic about prosperity in peacetime.

Under a series of bills intending to obligate the national government to maintain full employment, Congress was busy on what ultimately became the Employment Act of 1946. Public and private agencies were feverishly engaged in postwar planning. Included in these efforts was the recently organized Committee for Economic Development which, among several anticipatory postwar studies, sponsored the prescient work of T. W. Schultz, published in 1945, *Agriculture in an Unstable Economy.*

On the matter of off-farm migration, Professor Schultz's prescience was possibly aided by the fact that the 1945 data, noted above, were not yet available. Nevertheless, when the data showed a net off-farm movement of five million for 1940-44, as compared with 10 million for the two decades — 1920-39 — it must have taken a bit of grit (even without being confronted with the 1945 data) for Schultz to write:

> This movement of people from farms has not yet spent itself. If a high level of industrial production and employment is achieved after the war, there are reasons to believe that agriculture will still have several million persons who will migrate to other occupations.[2]

But the analytical considerations of Schultz and of immediately following contemporaries were not concerned with predicting mobility behavior as such but with projecting the environmental characteristics of employment and earnings in the farm and nonfarm sectors, leading to the conclusion that farm people should be migratory.

Of the assumptions needed for making the projections, those relating to agriculture (indicating the prospect of continued underemployment and sustained downward pressure on incomes) were far less tenuous than those having to do with effective performance of the nonfarm general economy. It was easier to be sure that "there are reasons for believing that a decade or two hence the proportion of the labor force that will be needed to produce farm products will be considerably below present figures."[3] (The word *needed* perhaps ought to have been emphasized.)

Given the almost certain future of adversity in farm earnings and opportunities, would farm people respond rationally? Since most farms were small, self-employment enterprises, there was a far greater capacity, as compared with the payroll industries, to absorb underemployment. The amount of net off-farm movement varied from year to year (in addition to apparent wartime influences) and in a way that seemed contradictory to economic rationality. "Why do farm people leave agriculture when farm prices rise, and why do many of them return when farm prices fall?" asked Schultz in 1945.[4]

This question and its descendants and counterparts, together with the availability of evermore sophisticated econometric and statistical techniques in search of an exercise, have provided the basis for nearly a quarter century of theses, monographs, and journal articles. Using only rudimentary technique and a bit tremulous in the face of *quantitative* evidence ostensibly to the contrary, Schultz arrived at a conclusion that has only been embellished and elaborated upon by subsequent research, i.e.,

> Not prices, therefore, but the existence of job opportunities — the opportunity to migrate — takes people off farms or requires them to stay put. This suggests an important deviation from accepted thinking concerning price as a balance wheel in the economy.[5]

Turning to positive measures for the reduction of farm underemployment and the improvement of low earnings, Schultz emphasized two matters that also were to be long-term mainstays in the field: a *"National Outlook"* for all labor and "public investments in farm people, particularly in the young."[6]

Research in off-farm mobility by economists attained little momentum until the 1950's. However, in 1949 E. O. Heady did a production organization analysis under assumptions of technological advance in which he foresaw the likelihood that the technological process would continue to be "land embodying" and labor substituting.[7] He reasoned that slowness in labor adjustment was attributable to four categories of barriers to mobility: (1) lack of knowledge — the labor market was not effective in revealing comparative opportunities; (2) costs of transfer; (3) risk and uncertainty of returns; and (4) inflexibility of human capacities. Heady's recommendations for an "innovation-inspired mobility policy" were about the same as those of Schultz, except that Heady went one further step and advocated payments and loans to underwrite the cost of transfer.

In 1951, D. Gale Johnson reported on research he had done on the question of union restrictions to job entry and whether they retarded off-farm migration. He depended upon quite highly aggregated and somewhat obtuse wage differentials from which to infer that "labor monopoly" was not a barrier. Noting that other aspects of the functioning of labor markets, including minimum wage legislation and the uncertainty of unemployment due to business fluctuations remained for investigation, Johnson concluded as follows:

> At present, I would argue that understanding the failure of migration to achieve equality of returns to labor in agriculture and non-agriculture will come largely through analysis of influences indigenous to farm people and their immediate environment. Most farm people in low income areas may be ignorant of the economic opportunities existing elsewhere; most may have insufficient capital to permit a move; most may have so limited a set of experiences that they fear the transition to nonfarm life; many may feel strong family or community ties; many may have reached an age that inhibits seeking new experiences; others may reject the values and modes of living that they associate with nonfarm living. These are some of the possible explanations, but as yet no one has designed a detailed and acceptable research program that would provide us with new insight. The development of such a research program is one of the important challenges in the study of rural life.[8]

D. Gale Johnson was among the few economists to appear frequently on the scene of off-farm mobility and related questions during the 1950's. Part of his work was concerned with refining the comparison between farm and nonfarm incomes, from which, among other interesting findings, came a statistical demonstration that per capita money incomes of farm people did not need to equal nonfarm money incomes to realize full parity of real income. Because of differences in rural price levels, labor force composition, capacity, dependency, income tax payments, etc., farm people could achieve full parity in real income with only 65 to 70 percent of the nonfarm money income. Since it is somewhat tangential, the development of income comparisons will not be reviewed here.[9]

With respect to mobility, per se, Johnson reappeared in November, 1951, with an article on "policies and procedures to facilitate desirable shifts of manpower."[10] No one had supplied answers to the questions and hypotheses he had laid out the preceding February as being necessary to understanding why off-farm migration was failing to relieve the gap between farm and nonfarm incomes. Nevertheless, he proceeded as if the "analysis of influences indigenous to farm people and their immediate environment" was not really so important. His roster of "policies and procedures to facilitate desirable shifts of manpower" included the establishment of labor exchanges which would expand job information and obtain job placements prior to migration; also in his roster were financial aid to off-farm adjustment and better rural education (especially in the South and for Negroes) as a means of increasing mobility. Johnson noted the possibility of encouraging local employment in lieu of migration but concluded: "I believe that major emphasis will have to be in terms of shifting manpower to existing labor centers."[11]

Fragments of sociologists' research evidence concerning assimilation of farm migrants in urban relocation sites could have provided a basis for some of the new insights that Johnson had previously called for. But if economists read the sociological publications, there is no evidence that much impression was made on them. This may, in part, reflect the propensity of social scientists toward disciplinary provincialism; in addition, economists' interests were primarily centered on the income statistics of those remaining on farms and not on the welfare outcome of those who left.[12] The current economic hypothesis—that an accelerated rate of departure would mean faster farm income improvement—was reflected in numerous papers. This preoccupation with acceleration must have obstructed investigation of writings on assimilation, some of which could have offered insights as to why the net off-farm movement was not higher, and especially why the backflow to farms was so large.

Evidence that economists were prone to view the research horizon through a very narrow lens came in 1954 and thereafter when an agricultural economist ventured into research territory which had previously been left mainly to sociologists. Eldon D. Smith, working with associates principally at the Universities of Chicago and Wisconsin (including Professors Schultz and Johnson), did an analysis of the assimilation of rural migrants into Indianapolis. The work was submitted as a doctoral dissertation at Wisconsin, and an article under a nominal and not-too-revealing title (but for economists, a conventional one) was published in 1956.[13]

Smith's findings were rich with new empirical material. For example, "if potential migrants are ill prepared," as he found them to be, "for the social and occupational experience of urban life, it is unlikely that merely providing information regarding the

types of jobs that are available will materially affect migration."[14] He spoke of "figurative ingestion" but "lack of diges-
tion" with respect to Southern whites; he found other important
differences and interactions relating to performance and reception for Northern as against Southern whites and Negroes.[15] He
found that formal media, including newspapers and the U. S.
Employment Service, had no significant informational role – that
the only important sources of information were relatives and
friends.[16] "Nearly one-half (44 percent) of Indianapolis migrants
indicated they were dissatisfied to the extent that they were
hoping or actively planning to return to farming."[17]

In his article, Smith acknowledged the help of D. Gale Johnson. Yet, six months later, when Johnson gave his paper on
"Labor Mobility and Agricultural Adjustment," he declared:[18]
"I have nothing new to say about programs for increasing mobility." Then he cited two of his earlier publications and summarized their main points, including that "more adequate information about non-agricultural job opportunities should be available."[19]

At the same convocation, C. E. Bishop delivered a paper on
"The Labor Market and the Employment Service."[20] Bishop
had read Smith's work; he noted some of the same points as
mentioned above, and his text implies a responsive impression
to Smith's findings. Nevertheless, despite the Indianapolis evidence that assimilation problems were complex and deep-seated,
Bishop sustained the economists' preoccupation with "accurate
information" as a basic need for more effective labor market
functioning. One wonders why Bishop would say: "It would be
interesting to know the percentage of migrants that seek the
counsel of employment agencies in making migration decisions
and that are settled in urban areas with the guidance of social
welfare organizations,"[21] when Smith had just reported his answer was zero, at least with respect to the U. S. Employment
Service. In any event, this was neither the first nor the last of
Bishop's entries upon the scene of rural manpower adjustment.

Unaccountably, Smith's Indianapolis work did not seem to
make its deserved impact upon either sociologists or economists. For economists, the barrier may have been a basic dis-
interest in already migrated people; for sociologists, the barrier
may have been disciplinary insulation – Smith's work was not
embodied within the conceptual framework of their cherished

theorems. This writer has to acknowledge that he, too, though well impressed with the empirical findings from the Indianapolis study, did not in 1958 show much perception of their potential for guiding further investigation or revising conceptions of off-farm mobility.[22]

The prevailing and enduring economic premise through the postwar years was that, if *enough* labor would leave agriculture, the incomes of those remaining would improve relative to non-farm incomes. Aside from the expectation of less under-employment, the implicit assumption apparently was that reduction of labor input would reduce output, thereby raising farm prices and incomes. But the indexes of input and output were not behaving according to this assumption. Although the explanation was not actually so obscure, it remained for Heady in 1957 to state it formally and explicitly:

> A reasonable hypothesis is: the net effect of further reduction in the labor force, and of consequent increase in farm size for concentrated agricultural areas, will be to augment agricultural output for several years more before this labor decrease alone causes output to diminish in major areas of commercial agriculture.[23]

He then presented reasoning and scattered evidence in support of the hypothesis, the effect of which was to say that, as some operators leave, their land comes into more effective use, in larger units and with better management, thereby increasing yields; hence, the radically divergent directions of the indexes of labor input and aggregate farm output.

Heady's proposition was not disputed, but it seemed to have made little impact upon those who were impatiently expecting the massive off-farm migration to be matched by a substantial improvement in farm incomes. If conceptually combined, the Smith and Heady findings could have suggested the basis for a reformulation of the farm mobility hypothesis, for the evidence presented was that neither those who left farms nor those who remained were clearly gaining the benefits it was expected they should. Hence, mobility, per se, was not the appropriate tactical focus; *accelerated* migration was not the answer for either; and *facilitated* migration, to be helpful to both those leaving and those remaining, would need to be accompanied by adjustment assistance in their respective environments.

But when D. Gale Johnson and Dale Hathaway addressed the American Economic Association in 1959 under the program heading "Facilitating Movements of Labor Out of Agriculture," both, and especially Johnson, adhered to the old hypothesis. "The net reduction in farm population," said Johnson, "has simply not been enough to offset the combined effects of a rapidly increasing physical product per worker, low and declining income elasticity for farm products, and the low price elasticities of demand for farm output."[24] However, in addition to increasing the flow, Johnson did want to reduce the mistakes — he suggested a national labor extension service which, in addition to job information, would be concerned with career opportunities, training requirements, how to apply, the nature of the work, etc. As in previous papers, he emphasized improved rural education.[25]

Hathaway restated the by-now familiar migration-income hypothesis but in somewhat more explicit form, particularly with respect to the expectation that off-farm migration ought also to reduce disparities in agricultural incomes among geographic regions.[26] As regards *improvement* in intersectoral and interregional income disparities, Hathaway evaluated the evidence as negative, but he did observe that the income ratios could have drifted into a worse state of disparity had the massive off-farm migration not occurred. He noted also that the impacts of off-farm migration upon the nonagricultural sector had been minus as well as plus (the latter being the manpower supply to aid economic growth); on the minus side, he mentioned welfare burdens and a Michigan study which showed that Southern white migrants were a disproportionate share of prison commitments.

Although Hathaway's concluding paragraph was a bit cryptic, it did reflect a broad comprehension of the migration process:

> The total effect of the migration from farms has apparently been of value to both the farm and nonfarm economies. Therefore, it would appear that the nation could well afford some public policies to cope with the social and economic problems attendant to migration. Without supplemental forces it is unlikely that migration will, by itself, bring about a significant improvement in the position of agriculture.[27]

The Schultz perverse farm price-migration correlation dilemma of 1945 had really never been put to rest. A variant of it,

which apparently was never formally stated or argued but which
had wide implicit acceptance among many general and agricultural economists, was that government farm prices guarantees
were a deterrent to off-farm migration. In 1957 C. E. Bishop, on
the basis of data scarcely sufficient to support his conclusion,
declared that government price supports did not impede off-farm
migration.[28] His statement was ambivalent and could have in-
voked disputation.[29] Apparently it did not do so immediately
and possibly because he and Larry Sjaastad were soon to provide substantial evidence that short-run variations in farm prices
and in farm incomes (relative to nonfarm) were not influential
factors on decisions to leave farming. The occasion was the
appearance of both at the Iowa State University conference on
Labor Mobility and Population in Agriculture. Observing the
same perverse price-mobility correlation as had Schultz in 1945,
Bishop said: "Unless we can argue that the increase in farm
product prices provided capital needed to finance the transfer of
labor from farm to nonfarm areas, it is difficult to make economic sense of the relationship [i.e., the positive correlation] between migration and prices received by farmers."[30]

Using the USDA Series on net migration from farms
— 1920-58 — as a dependent variable, Bishop reported regression analyses with the ratio of farm and nonfarm worker
earnings as the independent variable, but the perverse correlation persisted. Another hypothesis was tested, i.e., "migration
increases when jobs become available even though during these
periods the return per worker in agriculture increases relative to
the return per worker in nonfarm employment." The regression
between off-farm migration and the percentage of unemployment
in the economy produced a fair correlation coefficient. And it
had the right sign — negative.

*When there is less likelihood of ending up in a breadline,
more people leave farming! When not being threatened with the
breadline, more of those who have already left will stay put!*
What else had Schultz meant in 1945 when he said " . . . not
prices . . . but the existence of job opportunities — the opportunity to migrate . . . "? What else did Heady mean in 1949 when
he spoke of "risk and uncertainty of returns" as a barrier to
migration? What else was implied by the facts Smith had found
in 1954, particularly that three-quarters of the migrants into
Indianapolis stated they had moved on the word of relatives or
friends? Surely the most important impression to be conveyed

through informal discourse was whether job chances were bad or good.

Sjaastad's research,[31] reported at the same convocation, also dealt with relative income and the level of unemployment as factors that might influence the rate of off-farm migration. His comprehensive analysis led him to conclude "the United States population is clearly becoming more mobile in an absolute sense, and, more importantly, more mobile with reference to relative income incentives."[32]

Sjaastad's perspective and findings on the relative influence of differential income and unemployment were stated as follows:

> While unemployment measures are strongly related to the rate of off-farm migration, only a weaker condition is found for measures of (relative) farm income. Here there exists a serious aggregation problem. One can plausibly argue that labor leaving agriculture is essentially facing a national market, and hence a national unemployment rate is somewhat relevant. Such is not the case for farm income measures. Because of the variability in crops and prices in space, national farm income need not reflect the income position of any one region. The South, for example, has about one-half of the total farm population in the United States, yet this is precisely the area most insulated from the effects of farm price changes over time. If off-farm migration was purely an income maximizing choice, a change in farm prices and income at the national level will not necessarily be accompanied by a commensurate change in off-farm migration. While one expects a strong link between (relative) farm income and the rate at which people leave agriculture, aggregation weakens this link — perhaps more so than in the case of the unemployment hypothesis.[33]

By disaggregating both relative farm income and unemployment rates to a regional basis, Sjaastad was not only able to find the relation to income stated in the above quotation[34] but he also discovered a further significant fact about unemployment. Of the two regions he used — South and North Central — the unemployment rate was more important in the South. This suggested that the unemployment rate also ought to be disaggregated, i.e., "the 'effective' level of unemployment as well as the variance of that level over the cycle need not be identical over all occupational mixes."[35] Adjusting for variance suggested that migration behavior in the South and North Central regions was the same, but the occupational mix was more varied in the latter. This cleared the way for an important conclusion: "Both the level and the variation of unemployment in those occupations most favored by off-farm migrants is substantially higher than is the case for the total labor force, which presumably accounts for the volatile nature of off-farm migration over the post-war business cycles."[36]

The 1960 papers of Bishop and Sjaastad were a major breakthrough. Others were yet to reinvestigate the economic rationality of behavior of farm people with respect to mobility. But, henceforth, those conscious of the state of knowledge in the field would do so with an acknowledged uncertainty constraint relating to the nonfarm economic environment. Through 1960, the national and regional data that had been used primarily related to changes of *residence,* obtained by USDA and the Census, from which changes in occupation were inferred. In the future, data on *employment,* obtained from Social Security records, would also be used. More sophisticated statistical and econometric methods would be used. Whereas Bishop and Sjaastad had demonstrated that the annual variations in *net* flow from farms were inversely related to the level of unemployment, they had not determined the extent to which variations in the net were caused by variations in the outflow, or in the return flow, or in both. It was a question of great significance. It would also be one of tactical utility if and when the government took on responsibilities either to facilitate off-farm movement or to guide and assist resettlement, or both.

In his 1959 paper to the American Economic Association, Dale Hathaway had observed:

> One final point should be made regarding who has migrated. The statistics discussed relate only to net migration, which is the result of movement in both directions. Thus some of the present agricultural population are persons who left agriculture and for some reason returned. Unpublished data from the Bureau of Old Age and Survivors' Insurance (Social Security) show that above one-third of the covered farm operators in 1955 worked off the farm in covered employment in previous years but were not doing so in 1955. Many of these farmers had higher incomes in their nonfarm employment than from farming in 1955. Apparently these individuals either found values in farming that overrode income considerations, or they were unsuccessful in making a transfer to the nonfarm economy and had to return to farming. Thus is it probable that even the high migration rates of the past twenty years do not reflect all the persons who would be willing to leave

agriculture if permanent employment opportunities were available.[37]

Perhaps unintentionally, in this statement Hathaway revealed both the data and the central concern of his own and his associates' future research.

This section will conclude with a discussion of the work of Hathaway and associates, using Social Security data on changes of employment. Before proceeding, it is to be noted parenthetically that others have used employment data—the USDA Series noted in Section II as well as Social Security data—in studies of labor market performance.[38] These studies have the general effect of corroborating the findings of Bishop and Sjaastad and of Hathaway and associates as regards occupational mobility between agricultural and other employment; but since they are mainly concerned with matters somewhat peripheral to present central interest, they will not be reviewed here.

The work of Hathaway and associates at Michigan State University has been reported as it evolved in several doctoral dissertations, bulletins, and articles. For present purposes, two publications will be regarded as updating and recapitulating this research.[39]

Social Security employment data are derived from one percent Continuous Work History Sample, maintained by the Social Security Administration; the subsample consists of those reporting farm employment in any one of the continuous years selected for study. Five classes of farm employment were distinguished:

1. Farm wage work only.
2. Farm self-employment only.
3. Farm wage work and nonfarm employment.
4. Farm self-employment and nonfarm wage employment.
5. Farm self-employment and nonfarm self-employment.

Off-farm job mobility was defined by Hathaway and Perkins as changing from any form (and any amount) of farm employment in one year to exclusively nonfarm employment in the following year; in-farm mobility was the inverse. A person previously reporting nonfarm work exclusively was counted as an in-farm mobile if he subsequently reported *any* farm work. Under this definition, mobility measurement does not require that a person change his *principal activity* for either form of mobility nor need he move his domicile to or from a farm.

Given the facts of extensive intersectoral labor force participation, as developed in Section II, it is apparent that the Hathaway-Perkins definition would tend to state magnitudes of job changing considerably in excess of the amount of occupational adjustment actually occurring. Along with those who intentionally left afticulture in any one year are included those who, for that year, did not have reportable incidental farm income. Conversely, among those who intentionally come back to (or newly enter) farming are those whose incidental farm income becomes reportable for the current year. With this definition, a person can be counted as both an off-farm and an in-farm mobile without ever changing his principal occupation or place of residence.

The foregoing comments are not meant to be critical of efforts to use Social Security employment data. Rather, they prelude a further elaboration of the facts involved in Hathaway and Perkins' quite all-inclusive concept of mobility. Others have questioned the use of the data and the authors have defended themselves.[40]

For social science researchers, inadequate data are normal, hence the major emphasis is on resourcefully using them. Even though the conglomerate of multiple-occupation and occupational-adjustment activity that the Social Security data measure remains somewhat uncertain, there is no doubt that exploitation by Hathaway and Perkins has been imaginative and that their analysis of continuous registry data has significantly advanced our knowledge of mobility and the related environment conditions as between the farm and nonfarm sectors.

Most prior studies were based upon departures from and arrivals to farm residences. Consequently, the implications derived basically related to farm family heads, that is, to self-employed operators. Shifting to employment data inevitably means also including hired farm (and migratory) workers and, consequently, higher mobility magnitudes. Moreover, since job-changing occurs without migration (whereas migration without job-changing occurs less often), mobility magnitudes would be further increased for that reason.

For the period 1957 through 1963, Hathaway and Perkins found the national gross off-farm movement to be 14.2 percent per year which was almost offset by an in-farm movement of 12.4 percent.[41] The small nèt migration gain as against large out- and in-movements is the major discovery reported in this research. Since most of the in-movers can be identified as having had prior farm experience, the general conclusion to be most readily inferred is: farm people demonstrate a considerable readiness to move but they find the off-farm environment disappointing and hence return. Therefore, to attain a higher net migration, the nonfarm environment needs to be made less inhospitable. Except for its focus on the returnee, this point is not an unfamiliar one.

However, for high gross mobility rates, the Hathaway-Perkins data depend heavily on farm employment categories that characteristically base their working patterns upon intraseasonal supplementary employment as between the farm and nonfarm sectors. For reasons not explained, Hathaway and Perkins set only their aggregate national off-farm and in-farm mobility rates in apposition.

When their national aggregate rates of off-farm and in-farm mobility *by employment category,* for the 1957-63 period, are brought into apposition, the comparisons are:[42]

Employment status	Gross-off-farm mobility rate	Gross-in-farm mobility rate
Farm wage work only	9.5	7.0
Farm self-employment only	1.8	2.1
Farm wage work and nonfarm job	47.3	39.3
Farm self-employment and nonfarm wage job	19.3	19.0
Farm self-employment and nonfarm self-employment	16.4	16.3
Total	14.2	12.4

These results seem to indicate that there is no net off-farm mobility by farm operators — only those in single or multiple job wage work contribute to net off-farm mobility. In contrast, Census and USDA data say that the number of farms and farm operators is rapidly declining. Moreover, by USDA estimates, the number of persons doing some farm work for wages has not been declining in proportion to the declining amount of farm work done by all wage workers — which is to say that the participation rate of wage workers has been falling.[43]

Clearly, there is need of reconciliation. Possibly, the explanation may lie in the persistent propensity of Hathaway and

Perkins to report their results in terms of *rates exclusive of magnitudes,* without explaining the base for rate calculations.

Even though the composition of the magnitudes of off-farm and to-farm mobilities, as discovered by Hathaway and Perkins, may be uncertain, the differentiation and association of these measures with respect to attendant attributes offer significant insights into the economic environment of occupational adjustment out of agriculture. The high point of these supplemental findings was that for most classifications of the off-farm employment shift, the income results were not rewarding. In their own description, Hathaway and Perkins found that:

> In each of the three periods of mobility studied (1957-58, 1958-59, 1959-60), more than 40 percent of those leaving farming in one year had lower incomes in their nonfarm occupations the following year. Indeed, the distribution of gains and losses was such that the average gain of all mobile persons in the sample was relatively modest. A reduction in earnings appears to be the major element in the decision of many persons who leave farm employment to return to it after 1 or 2 years of nonfarm work.[44]

The effect of this finding was to challenge the long-enduring and almost universally held assumption of a pervasive disequilibrium between farm and nonfarm labor markets and the related assumption that the disparity between farm and nonfarm levels of income was to be reduced and ultimately eliminated by occupational mobility.[45] Was what had seemed to be disequilibrium actually a form of "dynamic equilibrium"? The Hathaway-Perkins findings as well as those of Lowell Gallaway, also using Social Security data to study mobility of hired farm workers, suggested as much.[46] "Dynamic equilibrium," as a concept in this context, means that the typical individual — within the constraints of his environment — has reacted rationally and has done what he could to maximize in accordance with his available choices — but with realistic forces apparently not being what had been assumed.

The USDA study of residence locations in 1958 of all adult farm-born persons then alive found that one-tenth of those who had left farms to establish residences elsewhere had returned to farms.[47] This implies a low rate of backflow. Compared to the nonfarm-born who had migrated to a farm and whose backflow rate was 56 percent, it is small. Regionally, the backflow rates for the farm-born and nonfarm-born were as follows:

	(Nonfarm to farm) farm-born (percent)	(Farm to nonfarm nonfarm-born (percent)
Northeast	6.9	47.4
North Central	10.7	54.3
South	10.8	54.8
West	7.6	66.0

It appears from these data that the farm-born have much better success in staying away from the farm once they have left than nonfarm-born have in staying on the farm once they have come there. Viewing these movements as contributory to the farm population in 1958, returning off-farm migrants were 1,816,000. and to-farm migrants maintaining residence were 2,584,000. For those who are preoccupied with why the farm labor force does not reduce more rapidly, these data suggest that net inflow from nonfarm sources is more important than backflow from off-farm migration.

Except for the favorable inference that one may draw from finding that 90 percent of off-farm movers did not return, the USDA data say little of their welfare gains. In contrast, Hathaway and Perkins, finding that incomes did not, on the average, improve significantly and that 90 percent of farm-to-nonfarm job changers changed back again, conclude that welfare gains were unsatisfactory and that the mobility process is inefficient.

As a measure of change of residence, the USDA data are probably more conclusive than are the Social Security data as a measure of job changing. This is because most people have either a farm or a nonfarm residence, not both. In contrast, many of those employed in agriculture are multiple jobholders, with unstable and varying patterns of intersectoral labor force participation. Consequently, the Social Security data may be measuring job adjustment; but along with it, they apparently include much of the job shifting of regular (nonadjusting) multiple jobholders. Because of this and because of the peculiar definitions of off-farm and in-farm mover used by Hathaway and Perkins, net job adjustment is not measured. Consequently, this reviewer's conclusion is that the extent of backflow and the extent of disappointment experienced by those deliberately attempting a farm-nonfarm adjustment is exaggerated in the Hathaway-Perkins research.

Yet, there remains this contradiction: the earnings level of labor in agriculture (self-employed and hired) does not equal that of apparently equivalent labor in counterpart nonfarm employment; but when farm labor tried to capitalize on this differential, its success record was not good. Why?

A very significant finding of the Hathaway-Perkins research (which could only come from continuous *individual* data) was that individual earnings levels in farm and nonfarm work were highly correlated. They suggested the explanation for this was "a decline in demand for the nonfarm jobs for which farm workers, by virtue of their skills, typically are qualified."[48]

In commenting upon this finding, Gallaway suggested there was "nothing in such a relationship which precludes the existence of sizable artificial barriers to off-farm mobility . . . it can be argued that artifical barriers . . . would result in a consistent earnings differential between farm and nonfarm employment across all skill groups."[49] To know what he implied would require knowing what is meant by "artificial," and Gallaway did not say.

In their Rural Poverty Commission paper,[50] Hathaway and Perkins reported in greater detail than previously on component attributes—race, age, mobility with and without migration, distance of migration, relationships to metropolitan centers, and income level of area of origin. The general effect of the findings suggests two broad conclusions, the first of which is stated by the authors and the second by this reviewer; first, Hathaway and Perkins:

> Thus, the mobility process as it has worked would seem to operate to widen the income gap between commercial agriculture and the low income persons in farming. It would also appear to widen the gap between the Negroes and whites who leave farming, and between the income groups after they leave their farm jobs. Thus, much of the low income problem in agriculture may be transferred to rural nonfarm and urban poverty by the mobility process, rather than eliminate it.[51]

To which this reviewer, as a summary of the present section, would add: National, aggregative (or macro) studies of intersectoral environmental relations and mobility/migration responses to them have been nonadditive and only modestly informative. Had there been a strong public policy interest, research results (particularly if incorporating such micro-level studies as Eldon Smith's) could have been useful in policy formation and, perhaps, even in program design. However, one important lesson implicitly embodied in these macro-researches that seems not to have made its proper impression is that off-farm (out-of-agriculture) mobility is not a unitary phenomenon. There is no such thing as "the mobility process." Heterogeneities and divergencies exceed similarities, and they are obscured or cancelled out by overaggregation; the nuances that could become tactical levers in a public effort to facilitate occupational adjustment are measured only by in-depth studies of particular types of situations. We have had studies of this kind; but, as this reviewer has already lamented in the instance of the Smith study, social science scholarship seems not to have had the capacity, or the will, to make its studies additive, or to extract a fund of basic knowledge from them.

Perhaps, this outcome is not remarkable: social scientists have not agreed on the basic framework for such a bank of knowledge. Almost ten years ago, this reviewer tried unpersuasively to argue that mobility as such was not the basic question—if people possessed appropriate productive capabilities and if the environment (farm and nonfarm) were congenial to career employment (which is more than job changing), then individuals could and would take care of their own mobilities—i.e., society could trust them to make their own decisions as to when to move and where to live.[52] Actual behavior and the existence of human needs have not been made more understandable by the polemical theorems of economics and sociology. Failure to reconcile their exaggerated and oversimplified concepts of human rationality has meant that neither offered a useful model for investigating the basic question—how do people go about adjusting to a changing and unpredictable environment?

I judge the essence of the studies concerning the relative on-farm and off-farm employment environment to be in agreement on two major points:

1. American people of farm origins and occupational backgrounds have the propensity to be mobile; they are attempting to respond rationally to what they understand to be employment alternatives.

2. The "push" forces—compounded out of labor-diminishing farm technology together with willingness of farm people to adjust—have not been matched by "pull" forces in the nonfarm economy for the capabilities that ex-farm people have to offer, or have the abilities to offer effectively.

Polarity positions can be taken on the limited success of

off-farm mobility: (1) the level and composition of employment opportunity in the nonfarm economy have been variable, uncertain, and insufficient; or (2) ex-farm people were not prepared — in basic education and occupational training — for the employment opportunities available (including also the sophistication to market their capabilities effectively). The "truth" apparently is a combination of both deficiencies.

NOTES

1. U.S. Economic Research Service, *Farm Population Estimates for 1910-1962*, ERS-130, p. 23.
2. T. W. Schultz, *Agriculture in an Unstable Economy* (New York and London: McGraw-Hill Book Company, Inc., 1945), p. 95.
3. *Ibid.*, p. 86.
4. *Ibid.*, p. 89.
5. *Ibid.*, p. 101.
6. *Ibid.*, pp. 204-8.
7. Earl O. Heady, "Basic Economic and Welfare Aspects of Farm Technological Advance," *Journal of Farm Economics* (May 1949), p. 293.
8. D. Gale Johnson, "Functioning of the Labor Market," *Journal of Farm Economics* (February 1951), p. 87.
9. Johnson summarized his income comparison work in "Labor Mobility and Agricultural Adjustment," *Agricultural Adjustment Problems in a Growing Economy*, Chapter 10 (Ames: The Iowa State College Press, 1958).
   Dale Hathaway further developed the same concept in his *Government and Agriculture* (New York: Macmillan Co., 1963), pp. 33-35.
10. Johnson, "Policies and Procedures to Facilitate Desirable Shifts of Manpower," *Journal of Farm Economics* (November 1951), pp. 722-29.
11. *Ibid.*, p. 729.
12. The present writer made a few comments, along with some wrong forecasts, on the subject of 1960. See Varden Fuller, "Factors Influencing Farm Labor Mobility," *Labor Mobility and Population in Agriculture* (Ames: Iowa State University Press, 1961), pp. 32-35.
13. Eldon D. Smith, "Nonfarm Employment Information for Rural People," *Journal of Farm Economics* (August 1956), pp. 813-37.
14. *Ibid.*, pp. 824-25.
15. *Ibid.*, pp. 821-24.
16. *Ibid.*, p. 815.
17. *Ibid.*, p. 820.
18. *Agricultural Adjustment Problems in a Growing Economy* (Ames: Iowa State College Press, 1958), Chapter 10.
19. *Ibid.*, p. 171.
20. C. E. Bishop, "The Labor Market and the Employment Service," *Agricultural Adjustment Problems in a Growing Economy*, Chapter 11 (Ames: Iowa State College Press, 1958).
21. *Ibid.*, p. 181.
22. V. Fuller, "Opportunities and Limitations of Employment Services and Other Informational Aids," *Problems and Policies of American Agriculture*, Chapter 21 (Ames: Iowa State University Press, 1959).
23. E. O. Heady, "Adjusting the Labor Force of Agriculture," *Agricultural Adjustment Problems in a Growing Economy* (Ames: Iowa State University Press, 1958), p. 146.
24. Johnson, "Policies to Improve the Labor Transfer Process," *American Economic Review* (May 1960), p. 403.

25. *Ibid.*, p. 408.
26. Hathaway, "Migration from Agriculture: The Historical Record and Its Meaning," *American Economic Review* (May 1960), p. 379.
27. *Ibid.*
28. Bishop, "The Mobility of Farm Labor," *Policy for Commercial Agriculture,* Joint Economic Committee, 85th Cong., 1st Sess., November 22, 1957, pp. 437-47.
29. Bishop said that price supports had generated higher incomes which had helped underemployed farm people to finance migration when the opportunities for nonfarm employment seemed favorable, *ibid.*, p. 442. But farm price supports had reduced price variability and, in response to reduction of risk, potato growers had been found to increase output, *ibid.*, p. 443. (And, if they were to raise more potatoes, would they not have to remain on the farm to do it?) Subsequently in this section, the work of Winkelmann in respect to the relative income-migration hypothesis will be noted.
30. *Idem,* "Economic Aspects of Changes in Farm Labor Force," *Labor Mobility and Population in Agriculture* (Ames: Iowa State University Press, 1961), p. 44.
31. Larry Sjaastad, "Occupational Structure and Migration Patterns," *Labor Mobility and Population in Agriculture* (Ames: Iowa State University Press, 1961), pp. 8-27.
32. *Ibid.*, pp. 9-11.
33. *Ibid.*, pp.14-15.
34. That a weak statistical relationship between off-farm migration and relative farm/nonfarm incomes was, in part, a matter of the level of aggregation was confirmed by Winklemann in a report published in 1966. Using regression analysis and data for counties within Minnesota, he concluded (as opposed to Bishop) "that those policies which have the effect of raising farm income tend to maintain a larger number of people in agriculture than would otherwise be there"; however, "the rate of reduction was not dramatically sensitive to income." See Don Winklemann, "A Case Study of the Exodus of Labor from Agriculture: Minnesota," *Journal of Farm Economics* (February 1966), pp. 12-21. (Quotes from p. 20; the author cites other references pro and con.)
35. Sjaastad, *op. cit.,* p. 17.
36. *Ibid.*, p. 27.
37. Hathaway, "Migration from Agriculture: The Historical Record . . . ," p. 383.
38. Lowell E. Gallaway, "Mobility of Hired Agricultural Labor: 1957-1960," *Journal of Farm Economics* (February 1967), pp. 32-52.
    Idem, "Geographic Flows of Hired Agricultural Labor: 1957-1960," *American Journal of Agricultural Economics* (May 1968), pp. 199-212. (Gallaway used Social Security data.)
    Edward G. Schuh, "Interrelations Between the Farm Labor Force and Changes in the Total Economy," *Rural Poverty in the United States,* Chapter 12, President's National Advisory Commission on Rural Poverty, Washington, D.C., 1968, (Schuh has used mainly USDA employment and farm estimate series.)
39. Dale E. Hathaway and Brian B. Perkins, "Farm Labor Mobility, Migration, and Income Distribution," *American Journal of Agricultural Economics* (May 1968), pp. 342-53.
    Idem, "Occupational Mobility and Migration from Agriculture," *Rural Poverty in the United States,* Chapter 13, President's National Advisory Commission on Rural Poverty, Washington, D.C., 1968.

40. Edward I. Reinsel, "Labor Movements Between Farm and Nonfarm Jobs: Comment," and "Reply" by Perkins and Hathaway, *American Journal of Agricultural Economics* (August 1968), pp. 745-49.
41. *Op. cit.,* "Occupational Mobility and Migration from Agriculture," pp. 187-92.
42. *Ibid.*
43. *Supra,* section II, and V. Fuller, "Hired Farm Labor in the West," *Rural Poverty in the United States,* A Report by the President's National Advisory Commission on Rural Poverty, Washington, D.C., 1968, Chapter 24.
44. *Ibid.,* p. 203.
45. The implications of their findings on the central question mentioned above and related matters are discussed by Hathaway and Perkins, "Occupational Mobility and Migration . . . ," pp. 211. Also *idem,* "Farm Labor Mobility, Migration . . . ," pp. 351-53.
46. Gallaway, *op. cit.* See also discussion by Gallaway of the Hathaway-Perkins article, "Farm Labor Mobility, Migration . . . ," *American Journal of Agricultural Economics May 1968), pp. 353-54.*
47. Calvin L. Beale, John C. Hudson, and Vera J. Banks, *Characteristics of the U.S. Population by Farm and Nonfarm Origin,* U.S. Department of Agriculture, Agricultural Economic Report No. 66, 1964.
48. Hathaway and Perkins, "Occupational Mobility and Migration . . . ," p. 352.
49. See Gallaway's discussion of Hathaway and Perkins' article, "Farm Labor Mobility, Migration . . . ," p. 354.
50. Hathaway and Perkins, "Occupational Mobility and Migration . . . "
51. *Ibid.,* p. 212.
52. Fuller, "Factors Influencing Farm Labor Mobility," Chapter 3 in *Labor Mobility and Population in Agriculture* (Ames: Iowa State University Press, 1961).

5

ATTRIBUTES AND INFLUENCES IN MOBILITY

Almost every writing on migration or mobility touches obliquely, if not directly, upon the attributes of those who move — geographically, occupationally, or both — and what influences seem to bear upon decisions made. Behind these concerns is the belief, if not the measureable fact, that such decisions and actions do not occur randomly but rather as patterns of motivation and rational behavior.

Who moves and why are, for several reasons, more than academic questions. Local politicians and community leaders have occasionally wanted to know if future leadership were being drained away. Especially in the 1920's and 1930's, a subject widely discussed was the burden upon rural taxpayers of educating youth who would contribute the benefits of their education elsewhere. A broadly held belief was that migration took away the best educated and most promising youth. If so, perhaps it was futile or even contrary to local interests to improve the quantity and quality of schooling.[1] For receiving communities as well, the attributes and qualifications of incoming migrants are important; knowledge of these might stimulate governing authorities and community leaders to take positive steps to facilitate effective assimilation, or, less affirmatively, to anticipate problems.

Crude correlations between years of schooling and rate of out-migration sometimes did support the theory that greater education created the propensity to migrate. Not until investigators began to look into career plans of youth was it discovered that causation actually ran the opposite way—that those *expecting* to have nonfarm careers deliberately sought more education and conversely that those expecting to farm often felt little need of more than a minimum education.[2] However, since so few of the youths expecting in the 1950's and early 1960's that they would go into farming ultimately did so, the effect has been that of further depressing rural educational attainment, already notoriously bad.

An examination of some 1957 data from Wisconsin shows that the correlation between planning to farm and low educational goals was not unique to that particular occupation.[3] Two of the conclusions reached are directly relevant to this review:

1. Planning to farm or planning to choose other blue-collar or lower white-collar occupations tends to depress levels of concern with the educational means for higher occupational achievement, but choosing a professional or executive occupation tends to raise them.

2. The more receptive he is to new information, the less likely a farm boy is to plan to farm or to choose a blue-collar or lower white-collar occupation, and the more likely he is to choose a professional or executive occupation.

There is a massive research literature on rural schools, which includes qualifications of faculties, significance of curriculum, quality of teaching, achievement, attendance, dropout, and related matters. The findings on major points are not in conflict—the poorer the local school jurisdiction, the more inferior the schooling is likely to be, from facilities to attendance. In general, rural schooling is measurably below urban in average years of attendance and consistently believed to be lower in quality although this is not so readily measured. Rural high school students have been required to follow a curriculum, in vocational agriculture even in face of the small likelihood they would become farmers. The generally poor educational preparation of rural people for urban life has shown up prominently in the assimilation process.[4]

Have migrants been those with greater intelligence or aptitude? Several research approaches have been made to this question. In Pennsylvania, a sample of 974 male high school sophomores from rural areas was identified and tested in 1947. In 1957, when they were typically 25 years old, the individuals were contacted and interviewed. This proved to be a not highly migratory population—only 15 percent had left the state; one-half were in the same community; three-fourths were still in rural areas; and of the respondents having farm backgrounds, one-seventh were farm operators or managers and one-tenth were farm laborers. The migration that had occurred had no significant relation to intelligence scores, personality adjustment scores, prestige ratings of parents' occupations, or types of parents' occupations. Nor was amount of education correlated. The authors explained their failure to establish any selectivity influences on the basis that Pennsylvania is a highly urban and industrialized state. "Consequently, its rural population has comparatively easy access to urban centers without having to migrate. Persons living in rural areas of Pennsylvania may therefore have less to gain by migrating than would persons in less urbanized areas."[5]

A different approach and a contrasting situation in Indiana yielded the same conclusion as regards tests of aptitude. In a low-income county that had suffered considerable depopulation, aptitude scores of adults (16-30 years of age) were on par with national standards. The authors concluded: "These data indicate that the adult population in this low income area is not the 'chaff' left from transplanting capable people into more productive areas. The mean scores of this sample show that the average adult from Hill County has aptitudes to learn and profit from occupational training equal to those of the adult United States population."[6] In curious contrast, the aptitude scores of high school juniors and seniors were below par, especially in communications skills and conceptualizing ability. The authors suggest that the schools should do something about this!

Given the great heterogeneity in the composition and patterns of the off-farm movement, researchers have occasionally encountered selectivity differences among peers in the propensity to migrate. For the most part, however, the researchers have taken into account the heterogeneity and the epochal nature of the phenomena being observed and were cautious about drawing broad generalizations. The one unchallenged generalization is that the outmovement has cut deeply into the youth. This has meant that an abnormally aged population was left behind. Even in the poorest states, amount of education has been inversely correlated to age over the past quarter century. Consequently, even if there were no significant differences in education among peers at the time of migration, the post-exodus population still at home would, on the average, be less educated.

Sociologists have expected sociocultural attributes to play a more influential role than they apparently have. Sociologists also expect familial-kinship, social group, and community ties to have considerable influence upon staying or going. The fact that the government role with respect to information and guidance in this exodus has been virtually nil[7] should reinforce these expectations because those making decisions and moves have primarily depended on relatives, friends, and neighbors for information and advice.[8] When and if these influences induce migration (they could work either way), they would also presumably influence the choice of destination. There have doubtless been numerous peculiar locality situations based upon interpersonal relationships and common background. These were prominent in the Okie-Arkie dust bowl migration to California in the 1930's. In the literature, one of the most identifiable "stem-family" migration patterns occurred in the Eastern Kentucky Mountains.[9] Investigating both the neighborhoods of departure and communities of reception (which were principally two towns in southern Ohio), these researchers found a preponderance of family and social class cohesion.

Although this reviewer has not encountered formal research on regional differentials in respect to the extent and duration of *group* migration patterns, the scattered evidence suggests they have been — and are still — more characteristic of the South and the southern Appalachian regions. The current migration from the rural South to northern metropolitan centers apparently depends very heavily upon kin and friendship.[10] This is not a new pattern for the South; nor is it confined to Negroes. It is part of a cultural pattern of group self-dependence in the South as against individualistic self-dependence in the North.[11] Other group patterns that are partly regional and partly ethnic are to be found among Mexican-Americans and in the off-reservation movements of Indians. In the North and West, individualism seems to be otherwise dominant.

One can speculate that these group movement patterns have

selective implications for personality and character; but whether these attributes relate to significant differences as regards manpower adjustment and social assimilation is a matter apparently not well answered in the research literature on migration and mobility.

Sociologists have usually not contended that their social-cultural selectivity hypotheses were alternative to those to be derived from the generalized maximization theory of economists — they have only said that with given economic needs and opportunities, people will respond one way or another according to rationales that the economist chooses to exclude from consideration.[12] It seems fair to conclude that research has not offered substantial evidence in support of the effectiveness of extra-economic determinants — at least not in terms of quality characteristics within peer groups.[13]

Economic theory does not specify that the rural-urban migration should have centered upon individuals who were poor or upon areas of low income. The determining calculation, say the economists, is the prospective net gain — whether from a position of poverty or of affluence. Accordingly, one expects (and finds) that there has been migration from other than low-income farming areas.

Nevertheless, it is reasonable to assume that low-income individuals who have the physical ability to be mobile will be the most conscious of possibilities that they might do better elsewhere and hence will tend to move, informed or not, for better or for worse.

Both macro- and microresearch suggest that there has been poverty selectivity in the rural-urban migration. During the decades 1930-40 and 1940-50, the highest rates of net out-migration were in areas classified as "serious low-income farming areas."[14] Subsequently, it has been observed that out-migration from counties tends to be closely correlated with lack of industrialization.[15]

Within peer group samples, researchers have found that comparative disadvantage in employment opportunities, tenancy, small farm size, low family income, and related circumstances were associated with higher rates of out-migration.[16] This is a matter of some consequence to the social welfare of the country, for it is *a priori* evidence of welfare improvement.

As has already been noted, the only prominent, enduring, and generally proven inherent differential of the off-farm migrant has been its youthfulness. There are several ways of measuring and displaying this fact and its consequences. Age-sex pyramids of the residual population dramatically show the effect of youthful out-migration. Those drawn for rural farm populations show them to be relatively short in children under 4 and in adults 20-40; conversely, the rural farm population has excessive proportions of males in all age categories over 45 and of females 45-60.[17] As of 1960, the rural-farm population had comparatively large proportions in the age categories 5-20. By 1970, off-farm migration will have drawn a majority of these away. And with so large a proportion of those likely to be reproductive during the 1960's already gone, the pyramid of the 1970's and thereafter holds the prospect of having a slender base of youth and a massive top-heaviness in the ages over 50. In this connection, one also might recall the point previously noted, that is, if present trends continue, the majority of the gainfully employed living on farms is not likely to be engaged in agriculture in the 1970's. The prospective future therefore is a farm population of superannuated nonfarmers!

Another revealing way to view the relation between youth and off-farm migration is by cohort analysis. Using the national sample drawn for the lung cancer risk study which was mentioned previously, this has been done by Karl Taeuber.[18] Table 4, drawn from his study, sharply outlines the role of age in migration. Using the fourth column, that is, cohort 1903-13 as an example, this is how one reads this table: Of those born on farms in the years 1903-13 and still alive in 1958, 26 percent of those born on farms in nonmetropolitan areas had left the farm by the time they were 18; an additional 16 percent left between ages 18 to 24; 11 percent more left between ages 24 to 34; and 5 percent more left between ages 34 to 44. Of this 1903-13 cohort, 58 percent had left the farm by age 44; but of the total who left farms, approximately four-fifths had gone by age 24. Thus, differences by ages within the cohort are found by reading down the respective columns; differences in pattern among cohorts are found by reading across the rows; and differences associated with being farm-born in a nonmetropolitian area as against being farm-born in a metropolitan area are found by comparison between the two banks of rows. Several points stand out dramatically in this table: Off-farm migration has been consistently high to age 24 (with interesting possibilities of speculating about trends as between the metropolitan and nonmetropolitan seg-

Table 4 *Decline During Successive Periods in Percentage Residing on Farms for Native Farm-born Population, United States, 1958*

Type of farm, origin, and age period	Cohort					
	1933-1940	1923-1933	1913-1923	1903-1913	1893-1903	To 1893
	percent					
Nonmetropolitan origin						
From birth to 18	36	30	26	26	19	17
From 18 to 24	29	27	19	16	17	12
From 24 to 34	–	6	15	11	13	15
From 34 to 44	–	–	0	5	3	1
Metropolitan origin						
From birth to 18	24	23	28	27	30	21
From 18 to 24	31	28	20	19	12	16
From 24 to 34	–	13	14	15	15	16
From 34 to 44	–	–	0	2	3	- 1[a]

a. Increase.
Source: Karl E. Taeuber, "The Residual Redistribution of Farm Born Cohorts," *Rural Sociology*, Vol. 32, No. 1 (March 1967), p. 20.

ments); off-farm migration is virtually finished by age 34; of the 1933-40 cohort, as large an off-farm movement had occurred by age 24 (55 percent) as had occurred by age 34 in the older cohorts, indicating a trend toward leaving farms at younger age levels. But this youthful migration will soon have to come to an end, for the day cannot be far distant when off-farm migrants will more characteristically be leaving by ambulance or hearse.

The accelerating influence of military service in the Second World and Korean wars upon rates of off-farm migration is apparently reflected in the increases shown in the two younger age-of-movement categories for the 1923-33 cohort. However, the fact that the rates were subsequently higher, for the 1933-40 cohort requires another explanation, especially with respect to the increased proportions of those who made off-farm moves before age 18. The data appear to imply that off-farm migration has increasingly embraced more young families as well as young individual adults.

A complete explanation of the influences upon and motivations of individuals and groups in relation to migration decisions is a large task and one not essential or appropriate to present purposes. Our central purpose is to review the state of knowledge as to differential abilities and preparedness of farm-origin people to be assimilated into urban and industrial life. The evidence on this specific interest implies and supports the following relevant conclusions:

(1) The off-farm migration has not been selective as to inherent ability; nor, to any significant extent, has migration selection run in favor of the more intelligent and capable. Any deviation from neutrality on this point has been bound up in the career choice-educational complex. Whatever else it is that underlies this observed complex of behavior, the evidence says that a substantial proportion of those not intending to farm held more challenging ambitions than those who did, and that they were motivated to achieve the education appropriate to realizing that ambition.

(2) The modal population leaving farms, i.e., under 19, was young enough for further education and training. Those at grade school level have not encountered great difficulty in adapting to urban schools.[19] Those who had finished rural high school were apparently at some disadvantage in entering college or finding jobs in industrial employment. Those leaving farm work at older age categories have been less well educated, but they were entering the nonfarm labor market at an advanced age after having failed to achieve their first occupational choice. The research has not satisfactorily disaggregated and identified the influences of these and other significant factors with respect to capability levels and occupational achievement in off-farm relocations.

(3) The off-farm migrants have been poor—comparatively as individuals and from low-income areas of origin. Your reviewer has not found anything in the research literature which would suggest that this is attributable to inferior personal capacity. On the other hand, the silence of the research literature suggests important inferences that apparently have never been investigated. These include such matters as obstructions of poverty upon the extent of migration, the thoroughness of search

for first postmigration job, and mobility after first postmigration job. It seems reasonable to suppose that, for heads of families who are at mid-career ages and with limited work experience, poverty in itself must have been an incapacitating factor, but the research literature says virtually nothing about this.

(4) Off-farm migrants, especially those past youth, have been under severe disabilities in the marketing of their labor services. First, there is the matter of inferior governmental labor market information in rural areas, a deficiency often recognized and commented upon. Second is the matter of being "informed" by relatives, friends, and neighbors upon whether to move or not to move, where to go, what kind of work to look for, and where to find it. This kind of "information" must have had a tremendous influence in directing migrants toward blue-collar occupations and particular locations and keeping them there. Yet, there are only a few instances of researchers (as distinguished from those commenting on research needs or just broadly theorizing) being aware that information might be important and even fewer who tried to analyze in any detail its influence upon assimilation.[20] Good information or bad, its impact upon distance and direction of movement and upon initial and subsequent job searches plus the overlying constraints of poverty upon all of these important factors, all are questions on which the research literature offers little help.

NOTES

1. Ronald G. Klietsch, *The Impact of Population Change on Rural Community Life, The School System,* Iowa State University, Agricultural Extension Service (Ames, 1962).
2. Archibald O. Haller, "The Influence of Planning to Enter Farming on Plans to Attend College," *Rural Sociology,* Vol. 22, No. 2 (June 1957), pp. 137-41.
   Lee G. Burchinal, "Differences in Educational and Occupational Aspirations of Farm, Small-town and City Boys," *Rural Sociology,* Vol. 26, No. 2 (June 1961), pp. 107-21.
   Lee G. Burchinal, A.O. Haller, and Marvin J. Taves, *Career Choices of Rural Youth in a Changing Society,* Minnesota Agricultural Experiment Station Bulletin 458 (Minneapolis, 1962).
   Donald R. Kaldor, Eber Eldridge, Lee G. Burchinal, and T. W. Arthur, *Occupational Plans of Iowa Farm Boys,* Iowa Agricultural and Home Economics Research Bulletin 508 (Ames, 1962).
3. Archibald O. Haller and William H. Sewell, "Occupational Choices of Wisconsin Farm Boys," *Rural Sociology,* Vol. 32, No.1 (March 1967), pp. 37-55.
4. U.S. Department of Health, Education, and Welfare, *Rural Youth in Crisis,* Part II, 1965.

The People Left Behind, Chapter 5, Report of the President's National Advisory Committee on Rural Poverty (Washington, D.C., 1967).

5. Harold Brown and Roy C. Buck, *Factors Associated with the Migrant Status of Young Adult Males from Rural Pennsylvania,* Pennsylvania Agricultural Experiment Station Bulletin 676 (University Park, 1961).
6. H. Neil Rude and M. R. Janssen, "Aptitude Tests Show Hope and Problems for Low Income Areas," *Economic and Marketing Information* (Lafayette: Purdue University Press, 1964). (Hill County is an assumed name.)
7. *The People Left Behind, op.cit.,* Chapter 4.
8. Charles Tilly, *Migration to an American City,* University of Delaware, Agricultural Experiment Station and Division of Urban Affairs (Newark, 1965).
9. James S. Brown, Harry K. Schwartzweller, and Joseph J. Mangalam, "Kentucky Mountain Migration and Stem-family: An American Variation on a Theme by Le Play," *Rural Sociology,* Vol. 28, No. 1 (March 1963), pp. 48-69.
10. Ben H. Bagdikian, "The Black Immigrants," *The Saturday Evening Post,* July 15, 1967.
11. James Sydney Slotkin, *From Field to Factory* (Glencoe, Illinois: The Free Press, 1960).
12. J. Allan Beegle, "Sociological Aspects of Changes in Farm Labor Force," *Labor Mobility and Population in Agriculture* (Ames: Iowa State University Press, 1961), pp. 73-81.
13. "Whether migration (all internal migration) selects the most able, or the least able, or both, or simply a cross section . . . remains a question on which no clear answer can be given." See Conrad Taeuber, "Economic and Social Implications of Internal Migration in the United States," *Journal of Farm Economics* (December 1959), p. 1149.
14. Gladys K. Bowles, *Net Migration from the Rural-Farm Population, 1940-1950,* U.S. Department of Agriculture Statistical Bulletin No. 176, 1956.
15. Allan Beagle, Douglas Marshall, and Rodger Rice, *Selected Factors Related to County Migration, 1940-50 and 1950-60,* Michigan Agricultural Experiment Station, North Central Regional Research Publication 147 (East Lansing, 1963).
16. Joe A. Martin, Off-Farm Migration: *Some of its Characteristics and Effects Upon Agriculture in Weakley County, Tennessee,* Tennessee Agricultural Experiment Station Bulletin 290 (Knoxville, 1958).
    Andrew W. Baird and Wilfred C. Bailey, *Farmers Moving Out of Agriculture,* Mississippi Agricultural Experiment Station Bulletin 568 (State College, 1958).
    William Metzler and J. L. Charlton, *Employment and Underemployment of Rural People in the Ozarks,* Arkansas Agricultural Experiment Station Bulletin 604 (Fayetteville, 1958).
    Dale E. Hathaway, "Migration from Agriculture: The Historical Record and Its Meaning," *American Economic Review* (May 1960), p. 379.
17. U.S. Department of Health, Education, and Welfare, *op. cit.*
18. Karl E. Taeuber, "The Residual Redistribution of Farm-Born Cohorts," *Rural Sociology,* Vol. 32, No. 1 (March 1967), pp. 20-36.
19. Burchinal, "How Do Farm Families Adjust to City Life," *Iowa Farm Science* (1963), p. 17.
20. Tilly, *op. cit.*
    Eldon D. Smith, "Nonfarm Employment Information for Rural People," *Journal of Farm Economics,* Vol. XXXVIII, No. 3 (August 1956), pp. 813-27.

6

DIFFERENTIAL MOBILITY BY ETHNIC GROUPS AND REGIONS

Of the manifold aspects of population redistribution in the past three decades, the desouthernization and urbanization of the Negro is the most remarkable. In 1940 a little more than one-third of all United States Negroes lived on farms in 15 southern states; by 1960 that proportion had declined to 7.5 percent, and one can safely guess that the 1970 Census is not likely to report much more than 3 percent. The proportions of the total Negro population remaining in the rural nonfarm and urban South has remained fairly constant, at approximately 15 percent and 30 percent, respectively. This means that the full and virtually direct complement of decline in the southern Negro farm population was urban growth outside the South. The nonsouthern urban Negro proportion more than doubled between 1940 and 1960—rising from 20.2 percent to 41.5 percent.

Cohort analysis by Daniel O. Price reveals that this abrupt change is attributable more to early mobility than to total lifetime mobility.[1] Each 10-year-spaced cohort for 1910-30 of southern rural Negroes had by 1960 lost at least 70 percent of its members by migration. But whereas the 1910 cohort had not achieved that level of out movement until age 50-54, the 1930 cohort had achieved it by age 30-34. The 1940 cohort was already ahead of that of 1930 as was also the 1950 cohort over the 1940. In less technical and more meaningful terms, this is saying that southern rural-born Negroes are migrating at ever younger ages — most of them now by the start of their occupational and reproductive lives.

As to migration, Price concludes that the contrasts between the southern rural whites and Negroes are as follows:[2]

> 1. Negroes move at higher rates, at earlier ages, and more likely as single persons.
>   2. Southern urban places and medium-sized northern cities attract southern rural whites to a far greater extent than they do rural Negroes; moreover, the propensity of Negroes to move to a large northern or western metropolis appears to be increasing.[3]

These findings relate to *rural net migration*. On the broader question of southern mobility in general (all population), Tarver points out that whites have been more mobile than Negroes. The main difference is that whites leave and enter the South (1955-60 data) in about equal numbers. In contrast, only one Negro enters the South for each three who leave.[4] For both groups, those entering are likely to be southern-born returnees.

Whereas the pattern of southern white migration to the North fans to the East and West and is widely diffused, that of the Negroes follows quite specific stem routes:

> Fifty-eight percent of Negroes born in the South Atlantic division and now living elsewhere, live in . . . Buffalo, New York, Philadelphia and Pittsburgh. Similarly, about 40 percent of the Negro lifetime migrants from the East South Central division have moved to . . . Chicago, Detroit, Cincinnati, Cleveland and Milwaukee. Finally, about 36 percent of the same group from the West South Central division live in . . . Los Angeles, San Diego, San Francisco and Seattle. Thus, not only have Negroes from the South, and by inference from the *Core* South, moved to large metropolitan areas, they have moved along clear-cut lines to their destinations, forming at least three major streams. . . .[5]

When a population cohort is losing around three-fourths of its numbers to out-migration by age 35, the depletion of the reproductive stock should soon result in a reduced capital population base, from which that migration must diminish. However, for the southern rural Negro, there is a considerable offset in high fertility rates. Whereas the birth rate for rural-farm whites tends to be two and one-half to three children per woman ever married, that for southern rural-farm Negroes exceeds four and one-half children per woman ever married. In contrast, southern urban Negro women average only three children.[6]

Since the southern rural nonfarm Negro birth rate is also high—only slightly below four children per woman—the total rural stock still remaining in the South has the capacity to produce potential out-migrants in substantial, though diminishing, numbers for years to come.

The rural Negro population of the Southern Coastal Plain, extending from Maryland to Texas, will apparently remain for many future years as the nation's largest single source of poverty-motivated internal migration. The technological and structural transformation of the cotton plantation is not yet fully achieved. Additionally, the growing of tobacco, mainly on small rented farms, which has remained principally a hand operation, is about to be mechanized. These and other impending changes will mean less employment and the disgorge of more already underemployed workers. As Kain and Persky have observed, the implications of migration from the rural South and the traditional concept of mobility in the United States are not in harmony.[7] The increasing difficulties of the ill-prepared rural migrant and the tensions of the ghetto are not appropriately subsumed under the erstwhile model of the individualistic foreign immigrant and the open opportunity of westward expansion. The southern-born rural person—white or black—does not ordinarily have much individual election as to attainment of educational self-competence. Consequently, the urban North has indeed had, and continues to have, a stake in the rural South—in its poverty and in the inferior institutions of human development that this region affords.

In contrast to the distinct urbanization pattern of the rural southern Negro is the indistinct mobility-adjustment experience of the Mexican-American. The obscurity and diversity of this population are such as to bar more than a few broad but quite meaningless generalizations: as a minority population, it is second only to the Negro; it is regionally concentrated in the southwest.

Why obscure and diverse? These attributes stem from the relatively open United States-Mexican border, both legally and illegally. In consequence, the United States citizen population of Mexican origin is freely aggregated and intermixed—physically and conceptually—with recent arrivals, whether permanent, temporary, or deportable. Given such an attenuated aggregation, the result could scarcely be other than incohesiveness, diversity, and conflict of interest. It is not too surprising, therefore, that public authorities have failed to respond to the educational and developmental needs of the Mexican-American. And, even though he may not have suffered prejudice and discrimination with the same intensity as the Negro, it seems scarcely worth debating whether this element has been slight or substantial in the compound of stagnating public impassiveness.

Individual scholars have long been interested in various aspects of the Mexican-American experience. The largest contemporary group effort was centered at the University of California, Los Angeles; its Mexican-American Study Project was conducted in the Graduate School of Business Administration under the direction of Leo Grebler. The project's reports emerged mainly in 1966-67, and have been perceptively reviewed, together with other related publications, by Niles M. Hansen.[8]

Anglo-Americans have a broadly and persistently held conception of the Mexican and Mexican-American as having peculiar abilities and motivations for arduous farm labor, especially when performed in high temperatures. Moreover, it also is widely supposed that they prefer to work intermittently, with ample opportunities for leisure. To the contrary, the evidence is clearly that these habits of employment reflect their limited choice rather than their preferences. Given the opportunity for development, the Mexican-American demonstrates abilities and motivations not unlike those of other people.

In the fifties and sixties, Mexican-Americans entering farm work (almost entirely as seasonal or migratory laborers) as their initial employment have found more opportunities to move out than did their elders, and accordingly have done so. This applies to recent alien arrivals as well as to second-generation citizens. Nevertheless, changes must be broader and deeper before significant relief is achieved in the underdevelopment and underutilization of the Mexican-American manpower potential. Even though aspects of rural-urban adjustments are involved, the basic element in adjustment is education and human resource development.

Of all ethnic group experiences with adjustment to urban life, that of the American Indian is unquestionably the most sordid. Until very recent years, governmental failures to promote economic development on reservations and to promote off-reservation employment have been equally abysmal. The all-time maximum of perversity in government Indian policy was achieved in 1953-58 when federal effort was directed toward termination and obliteration of tribal identities. Since the abandonment of that policy and particularly with the passage of the Indian Resources Development Act of 1967, achievements and prospects have become brighter.

In the past, social science research on the American Indian has not contributed affirmatively to public policy. Perhaps a stage of conceptualization is finally approaching in which the duality of Indian cultural and economic needs can be accommodated in constructive social science research. For contemporary details and perspectives, Niles Hansen has provided an excellent survey.[9]

The three above-discussed regional-ethnic situations of poverty and high fertility are the main remaining and potential sources of disadvantaged rural to urban migration. Additional, but not numerically large possibilities include the whites of the coal fields area of the southern Appalachians and (improbably) Alaskan natives.

Aside from these specific ethnic-regional situations, it is not impossible to believe that economic development may spread sufficiently to relieve greatly the need for massive or long-distance population redistributions.

Unfortunately, a great deal of what we "know" about population growth, decline, and redistribution by areas is over-aggregated, both in time and spatial units. Ten-year and inter-divisional comparisons can obscure many diversities occurring within time and area boundaries. And just as bad is the fact that what we "know" is not likely to be so by the time we know it. The Census-Social Science Research Council monograph, *People of Rural America,* a basic resource derived from the 1960 Census, had a 1968 publication date and made its library appearance in January 1969. This is the new efficiency of the computer age.

Using the July 1966 Census estimates of population by counties, Calvin Beale has discerned that many of the prominently held and influential beliefs, based on the 1950-60 Census data are now wrong. Contrary to prevailing beliefs, "completely or primarily rural counties retained their potential population growth much better from 1960 to 1966 than they did in the 1950's." Natural increase in rural counties has been less in the

1960's. But, "whereas in the 50's rural counties in the country as a whole had about 150 outmigrants for every gain of 100 in population, since 1960 they have had only about 20 net outmigrants per 100 gain in population."

Beale also discovered significant regional differences in this aggregate pattern of change. The four states embracing the Appalachian heartland, the Deep South Delta, and Black Belt had a net rural outmigration of one and a half million in the 1950's but only 164,000 from 1960 to 1966. Beale characterizes this as the most dramatic regional shift. But county data for 1966 revealed many surprising local rural growth situations — in the southern Piedmont, the Middle Tennessee Valley, eastern Oklahoma, western Arkansas — where heavy loss of population was the norm in the 1950's. The large region of continued population loss from nonmetropolitan counties is that extending from the Rio Grande northward through Michigan, westward to central Washington, and, thence, southeastward to the Rio Grande.

Beale concluded his discussion of recent changes in regionality patterns with the following observations:

> The general national picture that emerges since 1960 is a marked reduction of population loss — and even resumption of population gain — in many areas that have large numbers of the rural poor. This is not a backing up of population, stemming from lack of opportunity elsewhere, for it has occurred during a period of high national employment. The areas now having the greatest difficulty in retaining population are the vast open lands of the midcontinent, plus the mountainous Rockies. Here the mass of rural population is work oriented, reasonably well educated and housed, and unsaddled with an ethnic minority status, but economic and other attractions are apparently inadequate for population retention in nonmetropolitan areas.[10]

NOTES

1. Daniel O. Price, "The Negro Population of the South," *Rural Poverty in the United States,* A Report by the President's National Advisory Commission on Rural Poverty (Washington, D.C., 1968), pp. 13-39.
2. *Ibid.,* pp. 16-17.
3. However, some of the latter may transitionally migrate to a southern city. See: John F. Kain and Joseph J. Persky, "The North's Stake in Southern Rural Poverty," *Rural Poverty in the United States,* Chap. 17, A Report by the President's Advisory Commission on Rural Poverty, May 1968, pp. 288-308.
   Ibid., p. 292.
4. James D. Tarver, *The Rural to Urban Population Shift, A National Problem* Senate Subcommittee on Government Research, 90th Con., 2d Sess., 1968, pp. 17-18.

5. Kain and Persky, *op. cit.*
6. U. S. Bureau of the Census, *People of Rural America* (A 1960 Census Monograph), by Dale E. Hathaway, J. Allan Beegle, and W. Keith Bryant, 1968, pp. 92-93

Calvin L. Beale, "Demographic and Social Considerations for U.S. Rural Economic Policy," *American Journal of of Agricultural Economics,* May 1969, pp. 410-27.
7. Kain and Persky, *op. cit.,* p. 303.
8. Niles M. Hansen, "Urban and Regional Dimensions of Manpower Policy," report prepared for the Office of Manpower Research, Manpower Administration, U.S. Department of Labor, 1968 (mimeographed), Ch. 8.
9. *Ibid.,* Ch. 7.
10. Beale, *op. cit.*

7

ATTRIBUTES AND
INFLUENCES IN ASSIMILATION

Does the rural migrant make out successfully? How well does
he fare? Has the family adjusted to urban life? Although these
questions seem simple and reasonable they become elusively
complex when one attempts to make them operational and
meaningful for research purposes.

From whose point of view should the rural migrant be exam-
ined? One can ask the migrant or members of his family what he
or they believe and thereby try to obtain a *self-assessment*. One
can try to obtain objective data on occupation and employment,
level of living, community participation, and similar criteria and
thereby make an *external assessment*.

With whom should the rural migrant be compared? Rural
migrant versus urban migrant and urban nonmigrant in the relocation area? Rural migrant versus ex-peer nonmigrants in the
exodus area? Rural migrant before and after? All of these comparisons have been made, but nobody seems to be very certain
of what the results mean. The most usual comparison is rural
migrant (variously farm-born, farm-reared, rural-born, or rural-reared) versus urban (sometimes divided into urban migrant

and urban nonmigrant). The crucial question, it would seem, is whether or not rural-reared persons have bettered themselves by moving to the city.[1]

To whom and to what should the migration be considered crucial? The comparison posed as crucial is presumably less so for those who have already made the decision and the move than for those who are trying to make the decision. It is less crucial to program administrators and policymakers than the comparison of rural migrants with others within the relocation scene. For the public interest, it should not be enough to know only whether rural migrants bettered themselves or believed they had. Rather, if their capacity and performance were found to be inferior in some respects — education, health, training, etc — the need of corrective action to enhance capacity and improve level of performance would be suggested.

Some early studies of migrants found the amount of education to be not important to success in relocation; later ones say otherwise. In their first to third years of relocation, rural migrants can and often do present a near hopeless prospect of integration; after five to ten years, few traces of their rural beginning are to be found. Theorems about kinship influences that appear to hold for the time being in the Ozarks cannot be verified in Pennsylvania or Michigan. Residential migrancy and occupational mobility are no longer coidentifiable to the extent they formerly were, i.e., decentralization of industry and commutable transportation systems make job mobility more feasible without the need of migration; consequently, a great deal of unseen occupational and social assimilation can and does occur.

Leaving aside the specific environmental context of rural-urban migration and otherwise simplifying by omitting important variables, a streamlined two-dimensional research grid for the farm population only might be as in the table on the following page.

This highly generalized and oversimplified scheme fails to consider time from two points of view: (1) the specific time surveyed and (2) the amount of elapsed time that the subjects had for assimilation. Further, "exotic" situations — particular areas, ethnic groups, race — if recognized even minimally would greatly compound the design.

The foregoing exercise does not describe either what has been or exhort as to what should have been. It does lay out some of the possibilities that would have entered into comprehensive

| | | Type of Migrant | | |
Forms of Assimilation and Source of Evidence	Youth	Part-time farmers	Termi-nating farmers	Wage laborers
(1) Occupation and employment				
(a) Exterior assessments				
(i) Macroevidence*				
(ii) Microevidence**				
(b) Self-assessments (micro)				
(2) Community and social life				
(a) Exterior assessments				
(i) Macroevidence				
(ii) Microevidence				
(b) Self-assessments (micro)				
(3) Gains and losses: economic, social, and personal				
(a) Exterior assessments				
(i) Macroevidence				
(ii) Microevidence				
(b) Self-assessments (micro)				

  * national or regional impersonal data
  ** personal and local data

development of knowledge. Since individual pieces of research have only dealt with fragments of the columns and with either a collapsed category or a selected category of the rows, one recognizes immediately their limited power of generalization. Very little of what is known is (or should be) claimed as being other than a finding of that particular survey.

Occupations and Employment

There have been two national (sample) surveys of farm-reared people in nonfarm environments. The first, in 1952, was a by-product of political behavior research which was done at the Survey Research Center, University of Michigan.[2] The second (to which reference has already been made) was done in 1958 by the Economic Research Service, U. S. Department of Agriculture.[3] It was a by-product of research on lung cancer risks done for the Public Health Service.

The earlier (Freedman) study offers only quite general and cautious generalizations, which were restricted principally to occupational and social status. The farm-reared were found to be disproportionate in low-status positions, but the writers viewed this as not inherent in rural people. As newcomers to the urban social system, a marginal position was to be expected and was "likely to disappear in succeeding generations," they said. The Freedmans claimed their findings were "consistent with the hypothesis that farm to urban migration has provided a base for the upward social mobility of other elements in the population.[4]

The USDA survey is considerably more instructive. Its comparisons are between the farm-and nonfarm-born population, 18 years and older. Of 25.8 million native farm-born adults, only 9.5 million were living on farms in 1958 (sample: 35,000 households). As reported from other surveys, disproportions were found in blue- as against white-collar occupations. The nonfarm-born had approximately half in each; the farm-born was 35.5 percent white-collar, 60.5 percent blue-collar, and 4 percent farm workers. These relative proportions tended to remain fairly stable through all age groups, except for smaller portions of farm-born in farm work after 24 and until 55 years and over.

The ERS authors had a less esoteric explanation of the large blue-collar proportions than had the Freedmans:

> Logically, it is not surprising that farm people go principally into so-called blue-collar jobs when they leave the farm. The types of job skills that farm-reared people acquire, such as competence in construction work, or in operation and repair of machinery, plus the fact that they are accustomed to manual labor, suits them for work as truck drivers, factory operatives, craftsmen, or laborers. Furthermore their average level of formal education is often too low to make them readily suitable for many types of white-collar work without further training.[5]

Ex-farm people were found by ERS to be broadly distributed by industry classification. They were not significantly differentiated as to proportions of self-employment. They were unemployed at the same rate as others even though their labor force participation was a bit higher in the age 18-24 category.

These results on occupational achievement and employment from the national surveys will now be compared with those derived from some of the different kinds of the microlocality studies.

In Des Moines, Iowa, comparisons were made on the above-mentioned and other aspects of assimilation between farm migrants, rural nonfarm migrants, urban migrants, and natives.[6] As usual, farm migrants were disproportionally in the lower status occupations. Classified as "manual" and "nonmanual" instead of by color of collar, the comparative percentages ran as follows:[7]

	Manual	Nonmanual
Farm Migrants	57.7	42.3
Rural Nonfarm Migrants	49.8	50.2
Urban Migrants	37.1	62.9
Des Moines Natives	54.3	45.7

Variance analysis was employed to identify relationships underlying these gross differences. Individual occupational ratings (North-Hatt scores) were found to be closely related to years of schooling in all four samples, especially after high school. When schooling, age, and migrant-residence category were trichotomized against occupational ratings, migrancy was found to have no significant relation to occupational achievement. Schooling was the dominantly associated variable.

Median family income was lowest for farm migrants ($6,220) and highest for urban migrants ($7,360). Since the differences were the greatest in the older age categories, the authors believe this was due to the greater education of the urban migrant which made him eligible for continued advancement into higher paid job classifications.

Some employment-related aspects of migration and assimilation were considered in a Wilmington, Delaware study.[8] "Urban migrants more often came in response to a specific job offer than rural migrants did, while almost a third of the blue-collar workers from rural backgrounds stated 'other' reasons, essentially marking their dissatisfaction with their previous residence. Otherwise, rural-urban differences were not of any great importance. Work mattered to all categories of migrants, but specific job opportunities more often played a part in the coming of white-collar workers, and perhaps of the urban migrants as well."[9]

This unplanned looking for work characterized blue-collar versus white-collar migrants of all origins but was usually more pronounced for the rural blue-collar segment. Two-thirds of the blue-collar group had made no premigration trip to Wilmington or had come to visit friends or relatives as against two-fifths of the white-collar segment. Coming to Wilmington prior to migration in "preparation for the move" and "in connection with work" was characteristic of half the white-collar categories versus one-fifth of blue-collar urban origin and one-fourth of blue-collar rural origin. All migrants into Wilmington had depended heavily upon relatives, friends, and neighbors as against institutional sources for "aid or information." The outstanding category was blue-collar rural origin, of whom 86 percent listed this source of information and aid. The smallest dependence on friends, relatives, and neighbors was by the white-collar rural origin — 50 percent.[10]

The author summarized his findings on this point as follows:

> Formal structures, especially those built around work, do in any case seem to play a very large part in the initial contact of high-ranking migrants with the city, while less formal structures, especially ascriptive solidarities, do seem to be more important in the migration of low-ranking groups. Correspondingly, the high-ranking migrants take more extensive preparation for migration, accumulate more general information about their destinations, and get assistance from a wider variety of specialists. Such differences in the form of the migrant's initial relationship to the city surely affect his subsequent involvement in the city's life.[11]

A self-assessment approach was used in Racine, Wisconsin "for a test of 12 general hypotheses derived from a theory of value assimilation." The comparison was migrant Mexican-Americans versus an Anglo residence group.[12] It appears that more than half of the Mexican-Americans believed that the changes in their life after settling in Racine were "good"; the proportion was a little higher for the few Anglos who had migrated. Since a large majority of the Mexican-Americans had come to Racine for "work-oriented reasons" (like looking for a job?) and half the Anglos who migrated to Racine stated "family oriented, other" reasons, one assumes that the Mexicans had found satisfactory jobs and the Anglos were happy with their relatives.

In general, the Mexican migrants seemed to be assimilating well into the industrial structure of Racine. Occupational mobility from first job was equal for those starting in agriculture and those starting in the operative category. At higher levels of occupational mobility, Mexicans fell behind the Anglos. The

Mexicans had less favorable perceptions of change than were
held by Anglos with agricultural antecedents.

Very little questioning on abilities and performance of
off-farm migrants as industrial workers has been done of employers. Similarly, it has not seemed to be fashionable to ask the
worker directly and unambiguously about his nonfarm work
experience – his adjustment to a group work situation, to highly
specialized job divisions, to the foreman, to the union (if one),
etc. Scarcely any of those researching the field have tried to find
out about the process – how many changes of job, what on-job
training, what outside basic education or skill training – that led
to whatever occupational "status" the migrant had acquired.

The results obtained from a few of the inquiries made are
worth noting. A Kingsport, Tennessee, study[13] in 1955 at-
tempted

> to find out who made the better workers – men with farm or
> nonfarm backgrounds – we used three indexes: (1) length of time a
> worker served, (2) whether or not he ever attained a semiskilled
> position, and (3) in the case of farmer employees, whether or not
> his separation left him in good standing with the company for
> re-employment.[14]

Kingsport was then fairly recently industrialized within a pre-
dominatly agricultural area. The two companies involved had
grown rapidly since the 1920's and had used workers from farms
as one of their principal sources of manpower – approximately
one-fourth of the total in 1925-34, over one-third in 1935-44,
and under one-fifth in 1945-55.

The author summarized his findings in this paragraph:

> In only two cases was a significant difference observed between
> farm and nonfarm workers. (1) Of those hired between 1943 and
> 1946, 25 percent of the nonfarmers but only 13 percent of the
> farmers were promoted. (2) In the period up to 1937, there was a
> low but significant correlation (0.21) between those with farm
> backgrounds and those who stayed with the company ten years or
> more. About 79 percent of the farmers and 64 percent of the
> nonfarmers were in the long-service group. At no time was there a
> significant difference in standing between farmers and nonfarmers
> when they left the company. For the period as a whole, 81 percent
> left in good standing, the percentage being insignificantly higher for
> those of farm origin.[14a]

A more recent (1962) study in Michigan also found
differences in capacity and performance as between farm and

nonfarm workers to be negligible.[15] Twenty firms in Muskegon and Kalamazoo counties, with employment of 1,000 or more, were the base for a study of production workers, one-third of whom were women. All firms had some employees with farm backgrounds, but only six percent of all employees were currently part-time farmers.

The objectives of this study were:

> (1) To determine if industrial employers discriminated, positively or negatively, with respect to employing farmers simply because of their general attitude towards farmers.
>
> (2) To learn how the nonfarm on-the-job experience of farmers differs importantly from the experience of employees not associated with farming.
>
> (3) To determine the impact, if any, of labor unions on the employment practices of industrial employers in hiring farmers.
>
> (4) To gain insights into how to educate and train farmers to gain industrial employment.[15a]

It was found that employers tended not to be conscious that workers with a farm background might be different. Self-recruitment was dominant among production workers, whatever their background. Selection for employment involved no criteria unfavorable to farmers; part-time farmers were only told that they must accept and agree that the job came first. The majority of the firms had observed no difference in on-the-job progress, but 15 percent said that farm people had progressed more rapidly (on-the-job training generally prevailed). Some firms noted superior mechanical abilities and a more affirmative attitude toward work by farm people, but "there was no evidence that managers view farmers as a unique group."

Job vs. Social and Cultural Assimilation

Looking at the job assimilation in its simplest and least attenuated form can give one an exaggerated impression of how easily total assimilation occurs. In the Michigan and Kentucky situations reviewed above, very little geographic or cultural adjustment was involved. The Mexican-Americans coming to Racine had mainly moved from Texas and, hence, had made a considerable geographic change. But, as is generally their characteristic, Mexican-origin people are self-assimilating into particular types of work in which they have developed good working reputations and into their own preestablished *colonias* which appear to be what they did in Racine. In this sort of pattern, the culture is transported and consequently social assimilation within the *colonia* comes quite readily. Neither the distance of migration nor the social composition of the main city are of immediate relevance.

Negroes also have their own general pattern; for most, it is the long jump from the rural South to a major city ghetto in the North. Within the ghetto, as within the *colonia,* a restricted form of social assimilation can occur quite readily and with it a fair prospect of limited job assimilation. Temporarily at least, the Negro ghetto and Mexican-American *colonia* forms of job and social assimilation have a degree of stability. Less can be said for the southern Anglo, the off-reservation Indian, and the migratory farm worker—the latter comprising shifting elements of several ethnic origins. These several segments in their differing unfortunate situations, have not enjoyed even a temporary and limited form of job and social assimilation. In the short and the long run, they are largely uncohesive and peripheral peoples.

The foregoing observations imply that some elements of rural and off-farm migrants face a relatively uncomplicated assimilation centering mainly on the occupational adjustment of the family's principal breadwinner; in contrast, for others this adjustment is bound up in a complex of social and ethnic problems from which they cannot be readily insulated and which affect other family members as well as the breadwinner. As will be noted subsequently, the rural southern Anglo has had a quite singular set of adjustment difficulties deriving from particular cultural-ethnic attributes. In a parallel way, but for somewhat different reasons, job assimilation by ethnic-regional minorities and migratory farm workers has to take attenuating circumstances into account. In these two instances, perverse government policy has further intensified assimilation difficulties.[16] For reasons too well-known to warrant further comment, job assimilation by Negroes does not exist in isolation from a vast complex of attenuating factors, both current and historical.

Nevertheless, rural sociologists have believed there was something inherently particular or peculiar about people who have been rural. Consequently, they have spent countless hours attempting to find out whether rural-urban migrants were concentrated in particular parts of towns, whether they "neighbored" more or less, their church attendance, the organizations they belonged to, their voting habits, how many periodicals they received, whether they had a phone, how they made friends and who they were, whether they believed the results of their move had been good, in what social class they placed themselves and was it better than their parents', were their children having trouble in school, what educational and career ambitions did they hold for their children, and so on.

If the population sampled had a fair proportion of recent arrivals or had population elements culturally or ethnically exotic to the relocation area, there was a fair likelihood of finding some differences — even some statistically significant ones. Some authors have been candid enough to acknowledge that their discovered differences were not likely to prevail very long as the subjects in the sample had more time to adjust to urban life. Rarely has an author presented findings that seem to have any policy or program implications other than that the people should have been better educated. Otherwise, practical recommendations have been virtually nonexistent.[17]

Aside from the particular groups already noted — Mexican-Americans, Negroes, Indians, southern whites, and migratory farm workers — it can be said that, given their level of education, job training and experience, and age, the assimilation of rural-urban migrants has evolved about as one would expect in the open, fluid society of the United States.

At this advanced stage of the off-farm exodus, this reviewer does not see that a useful purpose is served in presenting a detailed account of the research literature on social assimilation. Moreover, since the problems of assimilation of ethnic-regional minorities are comprehensive and not particularly related to off-farm or rural-urban migration, the relevant and useful research comes in other contexts. Accordingly, it is mainly the southern white farmer and the migratory farm worker whose adverse situations fall more clearly within the rural-urban rubric and, therefore, warrant further discussion.

The work of Eldon D. Smith was noted previously.[18] He found that, of the rural relocatees in Indianapolis, Mississippi Negro migrants adjusted much better than did southern whites (from southern Kentucky and Tennessee). Moreover, some important differences showed up between northern whites and southern whites. This author's reasoning and findings on these latter differences are well put under the heading, "Satisfaction with Urban Opportunities Related to Social Adaptability to Urban Life," as follows:

Obviously the difference in day-to-day demands of urban existence and rural existence have resulted in differences in the customs and habits of rural and urban communities. The more individualistic habits of farm people, and their greater emphasis on hunting, fishing, and other non-commercial forms of recreation are familiar. Within the more heavily industrialized areas of the North, considerable interpenetration of rural and urban cultures has occurred through improved transportation and commercial and recreational activities. This has resulted in a great deal of similarity of customs and mores in country and city. Because of a much lesser degree of such industrial development in the South, this interpenetration is probably less complete, and, in addition, the cultural differences between the rural areas of the South and the urban areas of the North are magnified by the interregional (North-South) cultural distinction.

In view of this, one might expect that the change to life in a Northern urban community would require somewhat fewer adaptations for the Northern white migrant than for the Southern white. The Southern white migrant must not only adjust to a new job and a new set of housing accommodations; he must adapt himself to a new set of customs, a markedly different "kind of people."

The South, unlike the Midwest, was settled early by people of essentially homogeneous Anglo-Saxon culture. The waves of settlers of Dutch, German, Scandinavian, French and various other nationallity origins that swept across the Midwest bypassed the states south of the Ohio River almost completely. The rural areas as well as the urban areas of the North are to this day a mosaic of nationality groups. Thus, the experience of associating with people of dissimilar background, religion, habits, etc., is simply part of the process of growing up in rural areas of the Midwest and Northeast. On the other hand, in the South, particularly in its rural areas, there has been little opportunity for such experiences simply because the later immigration from continental Europe did not penetrate the region. The necessity of adapting to cultural heterogeneity and a changing cultural complex may have developed more highly in the Midwestern than in the Southern farmer the capacity for adapting to unfamiliar social situations.

Summarizing, as a result of experiences of the past that have been built into his culture, and over which he has no control, the Midwestern farmer migrating to a Northern urban center might be expected (1) to have a smaller adjustment to make and (2) to have a more highly developed capacity to make the necessary adjustment than does the Southern farmer. It must be emphasized, however, that if this hypothesis is valid, it constitutes no indictment of the character of Southern farm people. It merely means that these people who migrate from Southern farms to

Northern urban areas face somewhat more difficult problems of preparation and assistance in addition to employment information.

In general the hypothesis is substantiated by the study of Indianapolis migrants. Northern whites appear to be rapidly assimilated into the urban culture and soon lose their identity as migrants. Distinctive speech habits and other cultural factors identifying them as migrants are generally lacking. They make new friends more rapidly than do Southern whites and their capacity for making new friends among urban people and people from other regions also appears to be somewhat superior. Northern white migrants were not found grouped together in identifiable communities as were the Southern whites. Reports of employers indicate that they (Northern whites) are stable workers with no unusual rate of turnover, suggesting that return migration is not very important and that they have been able to adjust satisfactorily. They are reportedly quite easily trained to new skills, particularly mechanical skills. The fact that they are favorably regarded as workers is evidenced by the fact that the beginning wages of Northern whites in Indianapolis are significantly higher than those of Southern whites even after allowing the differences in educational preparation.[19]

Smith further noted that because southern white migrants had a propensity to return home after a brief period, "employers often regard them as poor employment risks for jobs requiring any substantial training period and consider them inferior workers for even unskilled jobs."[20]

Working with a less formal research design and contemporary with Smith, J. S. Slotkin also observed that southern whites had a great complex of difficulties in becoming socially and industrially integrated in a locality near Chicago and that there was much returning back "home."[21]

Why the outstanding lack of success in southern white migration has not been more challenging to researchers is difficult to understand. Those who tried to move and returned plus the much larger number remaining in place now constitute a large proportion of the white Americans in rural poverty.[22] They present a research gap, not seriously attenuated by issues of race and prejudice, in which something worthwhile could still be done. But at this juncture, considering the unresolved state of the "urban crisis," the relevant research frame would not be rural-urban mobility alone.

As regards migratory farm labor, the question of assimilation has been blocked by a pervasive fundamentalism to the effect that migratory workers had to exist because seasonal crop production needed them.[23] This sort of fundamentalism has afflicted researchers to the extent that most of their interests have centered on how to ameliorate the ordeals of migratory life rather than on how to eliminate the conditions that forced people into continued migrancy.

Migratory workers do not follow the sun with joy nor do they relish their poverty; when they have the opportunity to settle down, the evidence is they do so. They do not voluntarily become migratory workers because farmers have need of seasonal labor.

This heterogeneous population can realistically be looked upon as direct evidence of an assimilation failure in the American labor economy. A substantial proportion of migratory workers started out being off-farm migrants seeking relocation. Changes in the organization and technology of the plantation system which forced out tenants, sharecroppers, and wage laborers were the principal factors which promoted migrancy. Failing to find employment assimilation in place, they have had to subsist on peripheral quasi-assimilation in a system of semi-employment.

California is the scene of continuous efforts to settle down and become stabilized in a regular job and place of residence. Although we have virtually no formal knowledge of this process, the Okie-Arkie migrants of the 1930's have done well, thanks, to a large extent, to the tight labor market of the Second World War. Others of the contemporary migratory labor population are still trying to achieve some sort of stabilization. They face great obstacles, at the center of which are poverty and an elusive work base, which William Metzler has documented in a study made in Kern County, California.[24]

In this chapter we have been concerned with attributes and influences bearing upon success or failure in achieving assimilation. We have found that, by group and by area, widely differing results have been experienced. Can any general conclusion be drawn? The President's National Advisory Commission on Rural Poverty undertook to state one;

> The total number of rural poor would be even larger than 14 million had not so many of them moved to the city. They made the move because they wanted a job and a decent place to live. Some have found them. Many have not. Many merely exchanged life in a rural slum for life in an urban slum, at exorbitant cost to them-

selves, to the cities, and to rural America as well. Even so, few migrants have returned to the rural areas they left. They have apparently concluded that bad as conditions are in an urban slum, they are worse in the rural slum they fled from. . . . "[25]

NOTES

1. Lyle W. Shannon, "Occupational and Residential Adjustment of Rural Migrants," *Labor Mobility and Population in Argiculture*, Iowa State University, Center for Agricultural and Economic Adjustment (Ames, 1961), p. 126.
2. Ronald Freedman and Deborah Freedman, "Farm-Reared Elements in the Nonfarm Population," *Rural Sociology*, Vol. XXI, No. 1 (March 1956), pp. 50-61.
3. Calvin L. Beale, John C. Hudson, and Vera J. Banks, *Characteristics of the U.S. Population by Farm and Nonfarm Origin*, U.S. Department of Agriculture, Agricultural Economic Report No. 66, 1964.
   4. As a matter of fact, there is apparently a shade of truth underlying the proposition that the Freedmans call a "hypothesis" and which they speak of as though it were a highly shared and normalized one. Farm migrants are, to a limited extent, the successors of foreign immigrants with respect to providing a manpower base for the sustained growth of the industrial economy. But that comes by "the turn of the screw" and not by deliberate arrangements or destiny as the Freedman's impassive statement of their hypothesis implies. Apparently, this is not a generally accepted proposition, for other sociologists finding disproportionate numbers of rural migrants in lower status occupations seem to regard it as abnormal and implicitly unfair.
5. Beale, Hudson, and Banks, *op. cit.*, p. 12.
   In Kansas, two investigators had the extraordinary idea of asking in Employment Service offices about what farmers applied for when they wanted nonfarm work. The results, in order: construction, factory, truck driving, mechanical, retail trade, and machine shop. See John A. Schnittker and Gerald P. Owens, *Farm-to-City Migration; Perspective and Problems*, Kansas Agricultural Experiment Station, Agricultural Economic Report No. 84 (Manhattan, 1959).
6. Ward W. Bauder and Lee G. Burchinal, *Farm Migrants to the City: A Comparison of the Status, Achievement, Community, and Family Relations of Farm Migrants with Urban Migrants and Urban Natives in Des Moines, Iowa*, Iowa Agricultural Experiment Station Research Bulletin 534 (Ames, 1956).
7. *Ibid.*, p. 366.
8. Charles Tilly, *Migration to an American City*, University of Delaware, Agricultural Experiment Station and Division of Urban Affairs (Newark, 1965).
9. *Ibid.*, pp. 19-20.
10. This was not exclusive dependence (some had had multiple sources), but the dominant source over all was relatives, friends, and neighbors.
11. Tilly, *op. cit.*
12. Shannon, *op. cit.*
13. Clopper Almon, Jr., "Origins and Relation to Agriculture of Industrial Workers in Kingsport, Tennessee," *Journal of Farm Economics*, Vol. XXXVIII, No. 3 (August 1956).
14. *Ibid.*, p. 835.
14a. *Ibid.*

15. Ralph A. Loomis, *Farmers in the Nonfarm Labor Market,* Michigan State University, Agricultural Experiment Station Research Report 24 (East Lansing, 1964).

15a. Loomis, *op. cit.*

16. Reference is made especially to the role of the Bureau of Indian Affairs which serves as a catch-basin for that vast collection of ambiguities and venalities which ultimately denies the American Indian the possibility of being either an American or an Indian and to the role of the Farm Labor Service which, to guarantee the labor supply for seasonal crop harvests, has endeavored to keep migratory farm workers on the move.

17. For more ample (and sympathetic) discussions of the literature on sociologic aspects of assimilation, see George M. Beal and Wallace E. Ogg, "Secondary Adjustments from Adaptations of Agriculture," *Problems and Policies of American Agriculture* (Ames: Iowa State University Press, 1959) and Shannon, *op cit.*

18. Eldon D. Smith, "Nonfarm Employment Information for Rural People," *Journal of Farm Economics,* Vol. XXXVIII, No. 3 (August 1956).

19. *Ibid.,* pp. 821-22.

20. *Ibid.,* p. 823.

21. James Sydney Slotkin, *From Field to Factory* (Glencoe, Illinois: The Free Press, 1960).

22. Alan R. Bird and John L. McCoy, *White Americans in Rural Poverty,* U.S. Economic Research Service, Agricultural Economic Report No. 124, 1967.

23. Varden Fuller, "Economics of Migrant Labor," *Social Order,* Vol. 10, No. 1 (January 1960).

24. William H. Metzler, *Farm Mechanization and Labor Stabilization,* University of California, Giannini Foundation Research Report No. 280 (Berkeley, 1965).

25. *The People Left Behind,* A report of the President's National Advisory Commission on Rural Poverty (Washington, D.C., 1967), p. ix.

8

FUTURE RESEARCH RELATING TO RURAL MIGRATION: IDENTIFYING SIGNIFICANT AREAS OF INQUIRY

After an extensive review of the European, British, and American literature on rural migrants in the urban setting, a Dutch expert, Dr. G. Beijer, was unable to come to conclusions much more affirmative as to the state of knowledge in this area than is your present reviewer.[1] Beijer made several comments on the limitations of the research, two of which are as follows:

> Many of the studies consulted have a very static, fact-finding character. But, however valuable the categorizing and establishment of facts may be, the process of adjustment, of settling in, is in essence a dynamic one. Among the groups of migrants from the land a group of persons can always be found about whom facts can be collected, which in turn can be converted into social categories.[2]

Within the context of adjustment in the Netherlands, Beijer commented that:

> The extent of the problems that can derive from internal migration becomes most apparent in the matter of adjustment. Adjustment to the urban, often unfamiliar social relations in a technical

and industrial work environment can make heavy demands on the rural immigrant and, indeed, on the autochthonous population. The phenomenon of "adjustment" is now, by and large, a central problem of sociologists. But until recently the problem of the social integration of urban populations and, for instance the problem of the assimilation of migrants received comparatively little attention in this country. A few publications on adjustment problems of rurals in the city have appeared. But, as de Jong points out, mostly the sociological approach which makes use of the term "adjustment" does not take the relative nature of concrete situations sufficiently into account.[3] One result of this is that the relation between the person in the process of adjustment and the conditions to which he is adjusting is regarded in a manner that is too rigidly schematic and, in a certain sense, simplistic.[4]

With respect to the United States, Otis Dudley Duncan probably was implying approximately the same judgments when, at the conference on "rural to urban population shift—a national problem" held at the University of Oklahoma in May 1968, he said:

> I want to sound again the note that was first sounded this morning by Calvin Beale, that of disaggregation . . . (which) means putting your finger on the problem where it really is, and not burying it in some broad category like rural-urban migration. . . . The rural-urban shift is not a national problem, if it is a problem—it is a problem of some localities perhaps and some sectors. Indeed, it is not a problem at all nationally, but a great indication of economic growth. How else would we have achieved the benefits of the technological and organizational revolution in agriculture?[5]

Beijer's review of the literature from twelve European countries indicates that the profile of assimilation of rural migrants in all western industrial countries has some common characteristics. Assimilation in nonfarm occupations in the postwar period covered by the writings, i.e., until 1960-61, has gone quite smoothly. Factors not directly associated with the job and some not associated with income level have been conspicuous — especially housing, cultural differences, recreation, and related social considerations. Apparently, the smoothest transitions were made by the Scandinavians who are well known for their adjustability. At the other extreme were the French who had a basic problem of housing and with it cultural conflict. With respect to newly constructed housing, the French have considered whether

to separate inhabitants according to "social category and cultural level"—this in order to avoid isolation, estrangement, and
loneliness.[6]

As industrial and service workers, Italian peasants from the
South are reported to have proved capable and adaptable in the
urbanized economies of Turin, Milan, Genoa, Bologna, and
Rome. The minor social abrasions that occurred were mostly
due to the southern practice of doing outside many personal and
household chores that northerners believed should be done in-
side. Since most of the migrants were on the youthful side,
remolding their behavior and attitude came rapidly.

By 1950, most of the European countries, the United King-
dom, Oceania, and North America were sharing the phenomenon of a declining labor force in agriculture. Other nations,
including Japan, were still increasing in numbers, but most had
declining proportions of agriculture in the total labor force.[7]
Through the 1950's and at least into the early years of the
1960's, the tempo of the off-farm movement in the industrial
countries has undoubtedly accelerated.[8]

All European countries stand in contrast to the United States
in having earlier and more affirmative social policies, especially
as regards manpower training and retraining.[9] Farmers have
been eligible for these programs, and some of the trainees have
come from agricultural backgrounds.[10] However, of all industrial
countries, only Sweden can really be considered as having a
deliberate policy of facilitating the reduction of its agricultural
labor force through positive agricultural, manpower, and labor
market programs.[11]

Sweden's rate of off-farm migration has been the highest in
the world even though constrained by a housing shortage. Although the United States has not had facilitating programs and,
as compared also with Western Europe, has not had completely
full- or overfull-employment, its rate has ranked second to Sweden for most years. With their manpower programs, high-level
employment, and labor shortages, one might expect the European countries would have had comparatively higher off-farm
migration rates. That they do not probably can be explained by
sluggish land markets—those of Europe lack fluidity and have
numerous obstructions to land transfers, except in the Scandinavian countries. In contrast, selling or renting farmland has few
constraints in the United States. Consequently, labor and land
are more readily separable in Scandinavia and North America
than elsewhere.

Unless one wishes to probe deeply into values, motivations, and human responses, the reasons that people of industrialized, growing nations left the country at accelerated rates during and after World War II are not obscure or elusive. They are bound up in the forces of economic growth—in the declining needs and opportunities of labor on the land, concurrent with reciprocally rising manpower needs in the nonfarm sectors. Although neither of these developments may be universally viewed as a blessing upon developing mankind the facts of reciprocality and concurrency in the two sets of occurrences have indeed been a blessing. Without concurrent technological advance in agriculture, general economic growth would have been hindered. If technological advance in agriculture had not been matched by general economic growth, hence expanding opportunity in the nonfarm sector, who knows what state of despair might have been reached or what revolutionary consequences?

These comments are a prelude to the proposition that the western industrial countries have so far been very lucky in taking a basically impassive attitude toward one of the most major epochs of modern social change. The prevailing social and economic environments have been such that individual determination and self-dependence could absorb most of the obligations and solve most of the problems. In this luxurious situation there has been little demand for real knowledge of frictions and problems confronted in the adjustment process, including especially ultimate assimilation.

Perhaps this luck will continue, and knowledge in this direction can safely be left to the academy. To believe this or to accept it is risky. For several recent years, indications have been accumulating in the United States that its rural-urban labor transfer was not over—that not all assimilation was final, that the nonfarm sector was falling behind in absorbing the farm disgorgements, and that the gap between supply and demand in terms of preparation and need is widening. Moreover, a particular bit of luck for the United States has now run out, leaving the outlook significantly altered.

The "luck" referred to is this: In the decades immediately preceding 1940, the farm population maintained a comparatively high birth rate, while that of the urban population was falling. Hence, when the extraordinary labor demands of wartime and early postwar came along, the rural manpower stock came in handy. Or reciprocally, it could readily be assimilated—at least, temporarily and provisionally. In contrast, during the 1960's the economy has had to absorb the output of the higher urban birth level that began in the early 1940's. As is most visible in the troubled metropoli, the economy has not fully succeeded in absorbing both the abnormally large numbers of youthful entrants into its urban labor force and the rural-urban migrants as well. Consequently, pockets of poverty are backed up in rural areas, whose inhabitants at present have little prospect of relief either by migration or by remaining in place.[12]

The manpower exodus from agriculture is not yet complete. The diminishing number of farms is accounted for entirely by the elimination of low-income units. Between 1959 and 1966, farm units having a gross sales value of products less than $10,000 declined by over one million.[13] Contrastingly, those producing over $20,000 in gross value grew by 200,000. Small farms, rather than being abandoned, are consolidated by purchase or rental into larger ones. In 1966 there still remained 2,215,000 farms producing less than $10,000 in gross value. Economic forces and trends now well established will eliminate a considerable fraction of these 2.2 million within the next two decades.[14] It is not at all impossible that the rate of disappearance will accelerate due to the fact that present farm operators, especially those on the low-income farms, average near 50 years of age. Retirement rather than occupational change will take care of a considerable part of this yet impending labor force adjustment. An offsetting retention factor is part-time farming. The practice of working off the farm is growing (percentage-wise but not absolutely). In 1964 nearly one-half of all farm operators did some off-farm work and one-third of all operators worked 100 days or more.[15] As was remarked earlier, it has not yet become clear whether multiple-job holding by farmers will prove to be mainly a transitional phase of job mobility or, in part, a permanent occupational arrangement.

Summing up, this reviewer does not see the potential and remaining mobility adjustments of farm operators – in total and on the average – as being an urgent or highly significant area of mobility research; but this does not deny the existence of particular situations in which research related to farm operator mobility could advantageously be subsumed in a more comprehensive framework.

Hired farm workers, whose median age is 30 and of whom there are at least one and one-fourth million regularly in the labor market, although they are underemployed, constitute a prime category of clientele for human resource development programs and for whatever facilitating research would be useful. This is an elusive category, yet one probably manageable and identifiable for manpower program purposes; research should be concurrent and parallel with prospective and on-going programs.

Aside from these agricultural components, there are many human resource development problems in rural areas. However, one of the primary things to be learned from American and European rural-urban migration research is that identification by point of origin — that is rural, rural-born, rural-reared countrymen, or other variants — is not productive for the study of migration. Its lack of precision, the likelihood of heterogeneity in whatever population is being considered, and, most importantly, the findings that the rural environment has no more than an inconsequential, ephemeral influence upon human behavior in assimilation all argue that "rural" should be abandoned as a concept in assimilation and migration research.

Moreover, the usual concepts of migration and mobility have probably not added much to the perception of the basic and inherent adjustments demanded by technological change and economic growth. Whether in the mind of the economist or the sociologist, the thought process associated with these concepts is that of isolated adjustment toward equilibrium by individuals or a fractional component of society somehow finding themselves momentarily in a state of disequilibrium. As Beijer said, it is a quite static, simplistic perspective. The reality, in contrast, of modern dynamic life is that most people spend most of their lives adjusting to altered circumstances, new necessities, and new opportunities. Some of these adjustments involve geographic moves, and some of these geographic moves are from rural to urban places. So what? The fact of the geographic adjustment in itself has little importance and the fact of a concomitant rural to urban move, in itself, has even less. The basic and significant questions concern the environment of adjustment, that is, the nature and urgency of the demands and the preparedness of individuals to meet them.

What then, more specifically, are the prospects for useful research in the area heretofore identified, however imprecisely and unfruitfully, as rural-urban migration?

The first step is to recognize that this is not a separately identifiable or self-contained phenomenon. Rather it is an endogenous component of economic development attributable to the fact that economic development is uneven—from industry to industry, from area to area. When unevenness of development is interoccupational but not interregional, only retraining and job mobility in place are implied. If unevenness of growth were not interoccupational but only interregional, only mobility in space is implied. When unevenness of development is both interoccupational and interregional, combinations of job and place mobility are implied.

In contemporary American society, technological advance and consequently economic development are universally held as invincible goals; the necessity of occupational change and job mobility are therefore preordained. But the geographic question—where the economic growth shall occur—is not so predestined. Accordingly, whether jobs come to people or people must come to jobs is a question with latitude for decision-making. Heretofore, this latitude of decision-making has been exercised almost entirely by private entrepreneurs individually and collectively. The limited role of government at all levels in decision and aid has been overlaid with impassive accommodation to rival sectional and ideological political pressures. There have been no foresightful or responsible geopolitical considerations.

In more primitive states of transport and communication, there was a substantial element of economic determinism in agglomerations of economic activity. Today's location decisions have a greatly reduced amount of economic determinism (to the deciding entrepreneur). But excluded from the location decision (yesterday, today, and for how many tomorrows?) are the nonentrepreneurial private and public costs of agglomerating economic activities and their work forces.

In response, not to the magnitude of nonentrepreneurial costs in the present pattern of agglomeration but to the geographic mismatch of employment opportunities and the unemployed, the federal government has begun to assume a role. An index of the initial aggressiveness of this governmental role is reflected in the following statement (1967) from the Department of Commerce:

> An assumption of the study [of program planning for economic development] is that most (75 percent to 95 percent) of the required adjustment in locating people and jobs together will be achieved by the natural growth of the private economy. The area distress problem is a residual of these broad economic movements, and it is that residual with which Federal Government programs are concerned.[16]

The government posture reflected in this attitude, can scarcely be more than transitional, for its impassiveness is discordant with the complex of obligations already assumed by government and even more so with respect to additional manifest pressures that will surely evoke a broadened government sphere of action. Legislation already existing in full employment, manpower training and development, education, antipoverty, welfare, economic development, and related matters create a complex of obligations that require a more affirmative government posture as regards location. Bound up in this complex are questions of *where* shall obligations be discharged — shall the programs be brought to the people or the people to the programs?

Irresolution of this central question is serious enough with respect to presently existing obligations,[17] it cannot be avoided or long postponed with respect to two stridently demanding questions on which obligations are not yet articulated, namely, the ghetto economy[18] and public welfare policy.[19]

Perhaps the only feasible way to accommodate entrepreneurial interest, public interest, and individual interest is to resolve the first two in a range of situations — from rural open country to large metropolitan — thereby to offer alternatives to individuals who must respond to the dynamics of differential growth. Neither rural nor metropolitan America has to become or to remain a wasteland unless by impassiveness. Not every county can or should have factories; it is probably too late for every city to have much open space. Nevertheless, one can hopefully expect that there are opportunities for all situations, at least to avoid further deterioration if not to initiate substantial improvements.

For social scientists who are interested in the quality of human life in the technological age, these should be challenging times. There are broad environmental policies and programs to be formed; there are human resource development policies and programs already initiated which offer rich opportunities for experiment and analysis of experience. In contrast to the past when researchers implicitly accepted and viewed rural-urban migration as a self-contained, autonomous phenomenon, it should in future be studied in the context of its functional environment. Evidence of reluctance to migrate or of difficulties in assimilation can be given consideration in deciding between the need to migrate or the alternative of development *in situ*.

For significance and usefulness, future research ought to have the character of bridge-building — between identifiable groups having particular needs and the structural and functional re-

quirements and opportunities of the developing national economy. The relevant groups were identified in Section VI; structural and functional needs and opportunities are not so readily
identifiable or, perhaps worse, not so readily agreed upon.

This is not the appropriate place to try to develop a research
manual on the conjuncture recommended above. But a few
possible directions can be briefly mentioned.

First, is to learn from our doing. The current spectrum of
government programs provides more laboratory possibilities
than social scientists have ever previously known. Training and
relocation under MDTA (especially in the experimental and
demonstration projects), most aspects of war-on-poverty programs, EDA, and vocational education are instances in point.
However, I allege that we fail to approach anything like an
optimal level of learning from these programs—a hortatorical
comment on this matter will be made subsequently.

Second, a fair rostrum of research possibilities has already
been quite recently provided. Two sources have been mentioned: the volumes issued by the President's National Advisory
Commission on Rural Poverty, *The People Left Behind* (1967)
and *Rural Poverty in the United States* (1968) and the report of
the conference, *The Rural to Urban Population Shift* (1968) at
Oklahoma State University. *The Report of the National Advisory Commission on Civil Disorders* (1968) is not irrelevant. Nor
are the numerous recent writings on urban and ghetto problems.
Nor are the newly emerging writings on relief and income
maintenance policies. There is no scarcity of possibilities; only
the time and ability to sort them out are scarce. I want now to
return to and conclude with further development of the first
point—of learning from doing.

That research of academic orientation has failed to build a
body of useful knowledge concerning rural-urban manpower adjustments is a conclusion already sufficiently alleged, even if not
convincingly proved. Being convinced myself, I will further allege that impassiveness and the absence of a purposeful governmental role to aid the adjustment—at least prior to the early
1960's—are not entirely to be lamented. In retrospect, one can
see the basis of an obligation quite clearly and, as well, the
general outlines of what might have been done. Yet, that same
retrospective posture also provides the perspective to see that
had adjustment assistance programs been undertaken by government in the 1940's or 1950's, they probably would have been

badly devised, with the prospect of doing little good and possibly much damage.

The deficiency of useful knowledge is one reason for saying this. In addition, there is the matter of political ability and acuity. One has only to remember that prior to the enactment of the Manpower Development and Training Act of 1962, the federal statutes did not contain anything that clearly reflected a conception of the human being as a resource appropriate for development. Indeed, the statutes contained little to imply the possibility of any such thing as manpower policy. Policies and programs for developing land, rivers and harbors, electrification, farm technology, yes; for human beings, no. Without the concepts that have become politically respectable in the last half decade, prior ideas of how to aid rural-urban adjustment were vulnerable to miscarriage and frustration.

I can now move to further comment on learning from doing, with the MDTA segments dealing with Experimental and Development projects in worker relocation as a primary example. For learning purposes, these projects offer the prospect of a fruitful alternative to the aridity of testing academic theorems. The preliminary operating reports and evaluations from these projects indicate that significant learning is occurring, some of it so elemental that it seemingly should not have had to be learned by so organized an arrangement.[20]

Nevertheless, it is dismaying that the learning to be gained (or salvaged) from these experimental situations is apparently going to be so far less than ought to be possible. Failure to learn is not so much a matter of willful determination not to learn as of the constraints of role fulfillment. People who are managing programs, even experimental, and development or pilot projects, are inherently and inevitably committed to the successful *operation* of that program. Action programs of any type are scarcely conceivable wherein a primary sustainable goal can actually be objective research. The point does not need belaboring. One need only think of measures of accomplishment commonly set: How many were trained? How many moved? How many planning (or advisory) committees were organized? And so on. Administrative superiors, legislators, and politicians commonly expect answers to these kinds of questions. Seldom do they have much interest or patience in how much was learned about the subtleties of human behavior in response and performance under the particular actions taken, or to the possibilities of generalizing from one set of actions to other possibilities.[21] It is not entirely out of disdain for research that the "research" units of program agencies are kept mainly occupied with maintaining statistical magnitudes of program operation.

Given the nature of public enterprise, these constraints upon government personnel in learning from doing may as well be recognized as largely inevitable.

Conceivably, the social science academic community should be the source of an offset to this inherent deficiency. But it has deficiencies and obstructions of its own, and they are largely self-imposed. First, the academic discipline itself is fragmented, outmoded, irrelevant, and tyrannical. The disciplined academician approaches the problem or action site with a heavy baggage of theorematic and methodological paraphenalia. Moreover, academic disciplines have their own demands to be met, and often these are of high priority. The research has to be respectable, primarily in the eyes of colleague academicians, which means that problems have to be forced into the framework of tortuous disciplinary theory and into the cumbersomeness of complex methodology. Consequently, communication, cooperation, and complementarity between academicians and government personnel are impaired; growth of useful knowledge is suboptimum.

Significant research depends on willingness as well as ability to select significant areas of inquiry and approaches (even though not pretentious or elegant) that will be productive. And of course some lifeblood, that is, money, also is helpful. Rural-urban, migration-mobility research has not had a brilliant past in these regards; perhaps, in future contexts and settings, its counterparts will be more productive.

NOTES

1. G. Beijer, *Rural Migrants in Urban Setting* (The Hague: Martinus Nijhoff, 1963). (Published under the auspices of the Netherlands, Ministry of Social Work and the European Society for Rural Sociology.)
2. *Ibid.*, p. 19.
3. The author's reference is to P. de Jong, "De ontmoeting van de mens met de grote stad," *Sociaal Contact*, Vol. 4, No. 9 (Rotterdam, 1956), pp. 229-33.
4. Beijer, *op. cit.*, p. 180
5. U.S. Congress, Senate, Subcommittee on Government Research, *Committee Print, May 17-18, 1968*, 90th Cong., 2d Sess., 1968, p. 99.
6. Beijer, *op. cit.*, p. 230.
    Organisation for European Economic Cooperation, *Rural Manpower and Industrial Development*, General Report by Henri Krier, University of Reenes (Paris, 1961), pp. 93-96.

7. International Labour Office, *Why Labour Leaves the Land* (Geneva, 1960), pp. 9-10.
8. Varden Fuller, "Labor in Agriculture," *International Encyclopedia of the Social Sciences,* Vol. 1 (New York: The Macmillan Co. and The Free Press, 1968), pp. 236-41.
9. Margaret S. Gordon, *Retaining and Labor Market Adjustment in Western Europe,* Office of Manpower, Automation, and Training, U.S. Department of Labor, 1965.
10. *Ibid.,* p. 123.
11. Organisation for Economic Cooperation and Development, *Agricultural Policies in 1966* (Paris, 1967), pp. 475-81.
12. *The People Left Behind,* A Report of the President's National Advisory Commission on Rural Poverty (Washington, D.C., 1967).
13. These and the following data are from U.S. Congress, Senate, Report of the U.S. Department of Agriculture, *Parity Returns Position of Farmers,* 90th Cong., 1st Sess. 1967, p. 22.
14. This and following statements are not to be attributed to the U.S. Department of Agriculture.
15. U.S. Bureau of the Census, *Census of Agriculture,* Vol. II, Ch.5 (1964), p. 518.
16. U.S. Department of Commerce, *Program Planning for Economic Development: Some Implications for National Policy,* 1967, p. 9.
17. Jonathan Lindley,. Deputy Assistant Secretary of Commerce for Policy Coordination, Economic Development Administration told the Oklahoma State University conference on "The Rural to Urban Population Shift," May 17, 1968: " . . . I have not come here to propose solutions but to pose some of the issues which must be resolved if we are to attack the problem of carrying out a full employment mandate which includes efforts to balance the future location of people and job opportunities." Prior to having said this in his concluding remarks, Mr. Lindley had already not posed the issues specifically, categorically, or unambiguously. (Senate Subcommittee on Government Research, *supra,* p. 40.)
18. Jeanne R. Lowe, "Race, Jobs, and Cities: What Business Can do," *Saturday Review,* January 11, 1969.
19. Richard A. Cloward and Frances Fox Piren, "Migration, Politics, and Welfare," *Saturday Review,* November 16, 1968.
20. Early results from these projects were summarized by Audrey Freedman in "Labor Mobility Projects for the Unemployed," *Monthly Labor Review,* (June 1968), pp. 56-62. Later reports were given at a symposium on Worker Relocation on April 9-11, 1969, under the sponsorship of the International Manpower Institute, U.S. Department of Labor, the proceedings of which are forthcoming.
21. At the symposium on Worker Relocation above referred to, Gerald Somers, University of Wisconsin, commented more informedly on these and related aspects of suboptimal learning from the MDTA pilot mobility projects.